D1477043

GOLD

The *General Grant's*
GOLD

Shipwreck and greed in the Southern Ocean

Madelene Ferguson Allen and Ken Scadden

First published 2009

Exisle Publishing Limited,
P.O. Box 60-490, Titirangi, Auckland 0642, New Zealand.
'Moonrising', Narone Creek Road, Wollombi, NSW 2325, Australia.
www.exislepublishing.com

National Library of New Zealand Cataloguing-in-Publication Data
Allen, Madelene, 1942-2003.
The General Grant's gold : shipwreck and greed in the Southern
Ocean / by Madelene Ferguson Allen and Ken Scadden. 1st ed.
Includes bibliographical references and index.
ISBN 978-0-908988-37-2
1. General Grant (Ship) 2. Shipwrecks—New Zealand—Auckland
Islands—History—19th century. 3. Treasure troves—New
Zealand—Auckland Islands. I. Scadden, Ken, 1952- II. Title.
910.452099399—dc 22

Text design and production by IslandBridge
Cover design by Dexter Fry
Printed in China through Colorcraft Limited, Hong Kong

Dedicated to Robin, Bruce and Brenda Allen,
husband and children of the late Madelene Ferguson Allen

Contents

Appendices

Maps

Preface

Acknowledging that history is sometimes unknown,
sometimes embellished and rarely straightforward.

Charles Hobson

I first met Madelene Ferguson Allen (Ferg) when she was writing her book, *Wake of the Invercauld*, which was a voyage of discovery not only about her ancestor Robert Holding and his ill-fated ship, but also about herself: she was adopted and had been on the trail of her natural family and her identity all her life. I had been researching shipwrecks and the New Zealand subantarctic islands for a number of years and was at the time the Director of the Wellington Maritime Museum (now the Museum of Wellington City and Sea).

Ferg came to New Zealand and the Auckland Islands both by herself and later with her family, made many friends here and visited me at my home, where we talked Auckland Islands, *Invercauld* and shipwrecks into the wee hours. I was privileged to be asked to write the foreword to her *Invercauld* book, which was launched at the Wellington Maritime Museum.

We kept in touch and I was happy to be able to assist her on her next project, a book about the wreck of the *General Grant*. I was shocked to learn in an e-mail that she had cancer, though Ferg was typically matter-of-fact about her illness. She died on 13 August 2003.

Some time later I was approached by Ian Watt of Exisle Publishing, through Joan Druett, also a friend and a formidable maritime historian, to see if I could finish what Ferg had started. I readily agreed. Ferg's family generously gave me the green light and away we went.

I have found completing Ferg's book a longer and more difficult process than I had imagined. Even though we were friends and shared a passion for the subantarctic islands, we were very different people. I have tried hard to maintain the flavour of her writing and hope that I have done her work justice. At times I was frustrated by the fragmentary and sketchy details of the various proposed and actual expeditions to find the *General Grant*. Further research may have unearthed more detail on some of the expeditions but at some point a halt had to be called and the work published. The secrecy surrounding such ventures also makes investigation difficult. I hope this book will stimulate interest in and further research on the *General Grant* and that more information about the wreck, its aftermath and subsequent expeditions to find the gold may emerge.

Official files, newspaper accounts and personal interviews have been used to build up a comprehensive picture. It was sometimes difficult to track down Ferg's references. Although I have her research files, many references were in her head or in books on her shelf. If readers have difficulty in sourcing material, I am happy to be contacted. I take full responsibility for any errors of fact, omissions or wrong emphases in the book.

Ken Scadden

Acknowledgements

First, thanks to all of those people who helped Ferg but are not mentioned below. Please accept this as an acknowledgement of your assistance.

Australia: Berta Mansourian, La Trobe State Library of Victoria; Jane Rumbold, Monash University, Victoria; Jan and John Zelones, Western Australia; Robin Bailey, Melbourne; the Jewell family.

England: Mark Meyers, Bude Maritime Museum, Cornwall; Bryan Fred Dylan, researcher and diver; Esme Lucas Havens; Paul Havens; G.P. Dyer, Royal Mint.

New Zealand: Marianne Foster, Invercargill Public Library; Stephanie Gibson and Kate Button, Te Papa; Dr Anna Petersen, Hocken Library; Jeremy Cauchi, Trish McCormack and Alison Midwinter, Archives New Zealand, Wellington; Peter Miller and Aimee Brown, Archives New Zealand, Dunedin; Johannah Massey, Southland Museum; Wendy Adlam, Museum of Wellington City and Sea; Peter Attwell, Nigel Murphy Shona Beck and Joan McCracken and the staff of the Alexander Turnbull Library; Mary Rooney of the West Coast Historical Museum; and the staff of the Port Chambers Museum.

Bill Day, Conon Fraser, Malcolm Blair, John Dearling, Rosemary Tarlton, Joe Sheehan, Steve Locker-Lampson, Lynton Diggle, Dave Moran, Stan Kirkpatrick, Ian Church, Ruth and Lance Shaw, Duncan Somerville, Harry Goer, John Jones, John McCrystal, Bob Addison, Laurie Raines, Tim Galloway, Keith Eunson and Kristina Scadden-Gentsch.

A huge thank you to Ian Watt of Exisle Publishing for his faith, guidance and editorial support.

Macau: Tony Havens

Sweden: Emma Wising, Carl-Gunnar Olsson and Hans Orstdius, Swedish National Maritime Museum.

United States: Nathan Lipfert, Maine Maritime Museum, Bath; Christine Michelini and George Schwartz, and Dan Finamore, Peabody–Essex Museum; Tom Heard, Texas – a descendant of Aaron Hayman.

Special thanks to Conon Fraser for permission to adapt and reproduce the map of the Auckland Islands (page 47) from his book, *Beyond the Roaring Forties*, and to Mark Roman for creating the maps on pages 39 and 60.

Finally, thanks to Jack Duggan for permission to use extracts from three of his poems, 'The Islands of Despair', 'Then Came the *Little Mermaid*' and 'The *General Grant* Gold – And Those Who Seek It', first published in *Dance of the Stranger* (Moana Press, Tauranga, 1988).

Part One
Fact, Myth and Mystery

Old graves record the losses.
Old crosses count the drowned,
number the accidents; gloss over
the chilled marrow, the sickenings;
carve deep the dyings in grey weathered wood.

Jack Duggan

For over 150 years, the saga of the *General Grant* has tantalised and tempted. The tale, as all good tales do, has grown over the years into legend; its characters have become larger than life. But even after the facts are distilled from hundreds of newspaper articles, interviews and discussions, letters and reports yellowed with time, this remains a thrilling story of heroes and cads, heartbreak and loss, hope and despair. The ship, the wild ocean, the desolate subantarctic Auckland Islands, the plight of the castaways and the modern gold seekers – all these come together in a compelling narrative.

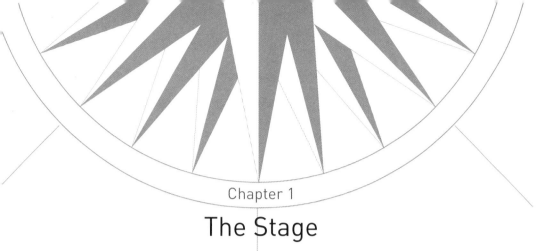

Chapter 1

The Stage

Without a doubt, the most important characters in this tale are the Auckland Islands. Desolate, wild, beautiful and forbidding, they are lost in the vastness of the great Southern Ocean, where the winds and waves sweep around the globe uninterrupted by any land mass. The largest, Auckland Island itself, is only 25 miles long and 17 miles wide at its widest point; fiords cut deeply into the eastern coast, leaving only two or three miles to a high saddle. Adams Island to the south, Disappointment Island to the west, Rose and Enderby Islands to the north-east and several islets make up the rest of the group.

The Aucklands are all that is left of two ancient volcanoes: Disappointment Island is the plug of the northern peak, Carnley Harbour the remains of the southern. The flat-topped hills rise to 2000 feet and cirque-crowned valleys run from the 'tops' to the eastern shore. The often fog-bound tops are a wild region of bog, rocky outcrops and spiky, cutting poa grass. To the west, the land plummets 1500 feet in a sheer wall of basaltic black rock to the sea. Their very location, between latitude 50°30' to 50° 60' south and longitude 166° to 166° 20' east, puts the Auckland Islands in what sailors call the Roaring Forties, the Furious Fifties and the Screaming Sixties. Even on the rare, relatively calm days, the long swells of the Southern Ocean surge in with all the force of the wide Pacific behind them, carving sea caves and overhangs. Only a few tiny sea-stone shelves offer the slightest possibility for a determined, desperate climber to reach the top and relative safety. There is an overwhelming sense of being on the fringes of the planet, utterly alone with sky and sea. In a storm, this area is terrifyingly dangerous: 'the waves build and build until they reach almost unimaginable heights. The highest wave ever reliably recorded – 120 feet high – was encountered there.'[1]

In the 19th century thousands of vessels braved the terrors of the Southern Ocean as trade and emigrants poured towards Australia and New Zealand from the Old World via Cape Horn, taking the route that mariners called 'dead men's road'. Many ships, broken and battered, arrived home, but many were lost without a trace in this fearsome ocean or were wrecked on the Auckland Islands because of faulty charts, the inability to take sightings, poor seamanship or plain bad luck. The names are still remembered – *Grafton*, *Invercauld*, *Derry Castle*, *Anjou*, *Compadre* and *Dundonald* – but only one wreck links those times with the present day; only one wreck takes determined dreamers into the wild waters of the west coast of Auckland Island: the *General Grant*.

Thirteen years before the American Pilgrims landed on Plymouth Rock a tiny ship called the *Virginia* slipped down the skids into Maine's Kennebec River. Although the nearby town of Phippsburg proudly refers to the *Virginia* as 'the first American transatlantic trader', it was in fact a pinnace – a two-masted vessel with eight oars. Even in those days of fragile ships, this was not one to brave the Atlantic but to tiptoe through sheltered coastal waters. This 1608 event did, however, mark the beginning of a shipbuilding tradition that continues to this day: the Bath Iron Works of Maine still supplies ships to the US Navy.

The young colony became a trading and a whaling centre and by the mid-1800s Maine's shipyards were known around the world for their quality of design and construction. Richard Morse operated his shipyard on Timber Island near Phippsburg until 1859 when he moved to the more vibrant port of Bath. His designs blended the smooth, fast, beautiful lines with a necessary generous cargo-carrying capacity and his ships proved themselves strong, well-built vessels. Following his death on 19 March 1872 the *Bath Daily Times* reported: 'Few men in the country have been more widely known in commercial circles than Mr. Morse. His ships sailed on every sea, and were freighted with the wealth of every clime.'

The American Civil War had been raging for three years when work started on the *General Grant*, named after the famous soldier and future president Ulysses S. Grant; Morse, a true patriot, had already sent the *General Butler* and the *General Shepley* down the slipways. Once she was launched on 23 January 1864, the Lloyds American Registry of Shipping described the *General Grant* as 'a Class A1 ship, built of oak, copper and iron fastened'.[2] She was 179½ feet long, with a beam of 34½ feet and a depth of 21½ feet. It is indicative of the number of ships being built at the time that her launch did not rate a mention in either the *Bath Sentinel* or the *Bath Daily Times*. Perhaps if it had been delayed until March, when General Grant became the commander of the Northern armies, more notice would have been taken of the event but, then again, she was just another new ship. The final cost of the vessel, after fitting out, was a relatively cheap $US81,166.88. Her homeport was to be Boston where, after her shakedown trip, she was handed over to Nathaniel Windsor & Co.

There has always been a debate as to whether the *General Grant* was a clipper ship. Keith Eunson, in *The Wreck of the* General Grant, [3] says not, but he perhaps took too narrow a definition of clipper ship. Contrary to common belief, the term covers a number of designs including the California clipper, China clipper, tea clipper, coffee clipper and opium clipper. The first three were ship-rigged vessels, with sharp bows, designed for speed. The coffee and opium clippers, also sharp-bowed, varied in size and might be schooner-, brigantine-, brig-, bark- or ship-rigged. The ships with the sharpest bows – those, that is, in which cargo capacity was most sacrificed for speed – were called extreme clippers. In the common vernacular, moderately sharp-bowed vessels were also called clippers. Medium or half clippers had a small cargo capacity but bows sufficiently sharp to make them fairly fast. A small proportion of the American California and China clippers were of the extreme type but medium clippers predominated. As Howard Chappelle has pointed out, it is almost impossible to generalise about clippers, but his summary is useful:

> As conceived popularly in the 1850s, a clipper ship was a large, ship-rigged vessel having a graceful sheer (an upward curve of the lines of the hull as seen from the side), a simple, high-arched stem fitted with a figurehead, a square or a round stern, rather low freeboard when loaded, generally a very sharp bow, and an extremely large sail area. The American clipper ships depended on proportion and line for beauty rather than on carving and external decoration.[4]

So was Windsor correct in advertising the *General Grant* as 'the new and first class clipper ship' for her first trip via San Francisco and Singapore to India? For her one and only trip to Melbourne, Henry C. Brook & Co.'s Australian Line would describe her as 'the magnificent first class packet ship'. The final word, however, must go to Nathan Lipfert, Curator and Library Director of the Maine Maritime Museum in Bath, where the *General Grant* was built.

> There were no true clippers being built in the US by 1864. The type only made economic sense during our Gold Rush and, some would say, at the height of the China Trade. By 1859 or so the building of clippers in the U.S. was over. Builders at the time persisted in calling vessels clippers, sometimes using the phrase 'medium clipper', but a modern maritime historian generally calls later square-riggers 'Down-Easters', because so many of them were built in New England, especially Maine. We have no information to indicate that *General Grant* had a sharp entrance and run, or any other attribute of an actual clipper. I would call her a Down-Easter, or stick to 'full-rigged ship'.[5]

By the time the *General Grant* had made her maiden voyage, around Cape Horn to San Francisco, then across the Pacific to Singapore and Calcutta, and had tied up again in Boston in September 1865, the word was circulating on the waterfront and in the taverns that she was a 'rough sailor'. To make matters worse, there was now the aura of death upon her. On 8 November 1864, as the captain's log, recorded, 'Mr. Merriman, Second Officer, while securing the starboard anchor fell overboard. Blowing very strong at the time with a mean sea, the ship agoing 10 miles an hour at the time.' Although the captain readied a boat, the first officer, 'being aloft at the time', reported that Merriman had disappeared. 'Under the circumstances, as I would have lost men and boat if they went from the ship . . . and there being no chance to save Mr. Merriman kept the ship on her course, and with much regret at the time.'

Before her next voyage, the *General Grant* was re-registered and sold to Page Richardson & Co. at a tidy profit of $12,900. Page Richardson then put her under the control of the Australian Line and announced that 'This splendid vessel is now in berth, and a large portion of her cargo capacity engaged and ready for shipment. Shippers may rely upon prompt dispatch. Fine accommodation for passengers in first and second cabins.'

Captain William Loughlin was a part owner of the ship so it was certainly in his interest that she have a successful voyage to Australia. It has been said, however, that she carried no passengers on the Pacific trip and Eunson mentions a report that she had no cargo.[6] Both these seem most unlikely. Although the main influx of emigrants and miners to the Australian goldfields had passed its peak, it would have been odd if she carried no passengers when it was clearly advertised that she had cabin space. There is no apparent reason that a ship would set out on this long and dangerous voyage without financial reward. Had previous arrangements been made in Australia for the ship to return with a valuable cargo that would make a less profitable voyage worthwhile?

Profitable or no, tragedy continued to haunt the *General Grant*. On 28 November 1865, the orders rang clear across the decks:

> 'Stand by to make sail! Set royals and flying jib!
> Man the royal halliards and sheets, flying jib halliards and sheets,
>   weather royal braces!
> Let fall! Sheet home! Hoist away royals and flying jib!
> Lay aloft and loose fore topsail!
> Lay aloft and loose the mainsail!
> Haul taut! Haul out!'

On 30 November, their second day out of port, as the wind freshened, young Rufus Tyler, the third mate, was on morning watch. But he never heard the noon bell, for in the action of shortening the sails he was lost overboard. More than 10 days later, on Tuesday 17 April 1866 the heights of Melbourne's Port Phillip Heads rose from the horizon. The *General Grant* had arrived safely in Australia.

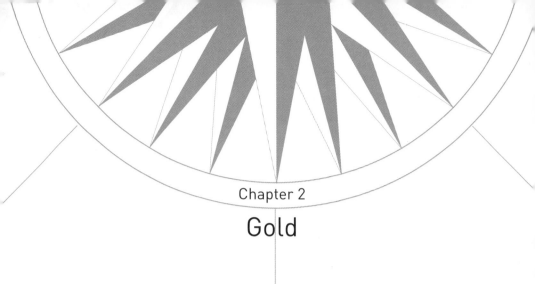

Chapter 2

Gold

In the mid-19th century hundreds of thousands of men, from all corners of the globe, flocked to gold rushes in California, the Klondike, the Yukon, Australia and New Zealand. Cries of 'Gold! Zolta! Goud! Egole! Aur! Arany! Kulta! Ouro!' echoed around the world in as many languages as there were countries that disgorged men from farms and factories and office desks to search for the elusive yellow metal. When the Victorian rush was in full swing in 1861, there were not enough vessels to carry all those who wanted passage to Australia. Shipping companies put their oldest hulks back into service, hammered slabs of wood into cargo holds for bunks, ordered new ships – anything to transport the diggers across the Atlantic and the Pacific.

Because the deposits were so numerous and far-flung it is impossible to give a precise date for the first discovery of gold in Australia. The first 'find' seems to have been a hoax. In 1790 a convict at Port Jackson told New South Wales Governor Arthur Phillip about 'an auriferous region near Sydney'. When the area was examined, particles of real gold dust were found. After the initial excitement and further investigation, however, it was discovered that the convict 'in the hope of obtaining his pardon as a reward, had filed a guinea and some brass buttons, which, judiciously mixed, made a tolerable pile of gold-dust, and this he carefully distributed over a small tract of sandy land'.[1]

One story tells of a shepherd finding gold while wandering with his sheep; in another a farm labourer dug up a nugget while putting in fence posts. In both cases, the finders mysteriously disappeared before they could tell anyone of the location of their discoveries. It will never be known if they were murdered, or perhaps bought off by local officials determined to keep their region from being torn apart, physically and morally, by a gold-seeking invasion.

In 1839, a Polish count, Paul Strzelecki, on a scientific exploring expedition from Sydney across the mountains into the region of Victoria which he called Gippsland, after New South Wales Governor Sir George Gipps, made some interesting discoveries. He sent his observations, maps and particles of gold he had found among decomposed ironstone, to Roderick Murchison, a geologist in England. On studying these, the latter noticed the similarities to the geological formation and gold-bearing rocks of the Ural Mountains in Russia. Murchison wrote to the Secretary of State for the Colonies, Lord Grey, pointing out the resemblance. Grey read the letter with considerable interest but filed it away.

A continued suppression of information about the presence of gold on the continent became unofficial government policy. The most widely recounted incident occurred in 1844 when the Reverend W.B. Clarke, an amateur geologist, showed his friend, Sir George Phillips, gold samples which he had found. Phillips is said to have commanded, 'Put it away, Mr Clarke, or we shall all have our throats cut.'

The felons, pickpockets and murderers who found themselves transported to Australia were not all kept under lock and key. Many were assigned to settlers, traders or various government departments as labourers. They were given specific tasks and a set time to complete them and if they finished by the deadline, they were allowed to work on their own account. By the time Grey received the letter from Murchison a new probation system had just come into effect where a convict was free to take what work he wished, but had to report on a regular basis. Grey knew that social chaos would ensue if thousands of convicts turned their backs on this tenuous arrangement and raced away to find gold. Governor Gipps, too, made it clear to Strzelecki that he was to say nothing. The count complied, and omitted the subject from his first book on Australia. Sydney officials refused to conduct a survey in 1848 when a nugget, found near Berrima, was brought to their attention.

By 1850 the California gold rush was in full swing and many Australians headed for the United States to try their luck. Among them was Edward Hargraves. His American experience was disappointing but he returned confident that with his newfound knowledge he could find gold in Australia. He headed off over the Blue Mountains and onto the Bathurst Plains. There he met John Lister, who guided him to the area where he had found gold some time previously. Hargraves, who never mentioned Lister's name, has gone down in history as the man who started the Australian gold rush with his discovery of gold at Summerhill Creek in February 1851. The Colonial Secretary put a brave face on it when Hargraves reported his find: 'If this is gold country, it comes on us like a clap of thunder, and we are scarcely prepared to credit it'. It seems most unlikely that an official in his position would not have known what was lying beneath the surface – literally and figuratively. The authorities would have been extremely short-sighted not to have made some plans for the possibility of a gold rush, especially since the social upheaval and lawlessness in California had been so well publicised.

Finally realising that the only way to stem the flow of men to California was to exploit their own gold, the Australian authorities offered a reward to the first person to 'bring in' a viable site. Hargraves's samples were found to be rich in gold and on 22 May 1851 the find was declared. He was rewarded with the £500 prize and appointed Crown Commissioner of the Goldfields. The rush was on. Despite his lofty position, however, Hargraves proved dishonourable, never giving credit to or sharing his fortune with Lister or the others who guided him to his first discovery. They sued him, but to no avail. Audacious about his motives, Hargraves wrote in his autobiography: 'it was never my intention ... to work for gold, my only desire was to make the discovery, and rely on the Government and the country for my reward'.[2]

Frenzy overtook the colony. As the Lieutenant-Governor of Victoria, Charles La Trobe wrote to Earl Grey in October 1851:

Not only have the idlers to be found in every community, and day labourers in town and the adjacent country, shopmen, artisans, and mechanics of every description, thrown up their employment, and in most cases, leaving their employers and their wives and families to take care of themselves, run off to the workings, but responsible tradesmen, farmers, clerks of every grade, and not a few of the superior classes have followed: ... Cottages are deserted, houses to let, business is at a standstill, and even schools are closed. In some of the suburbs, not a man is left and the women are known for self-protection to forget neighbours jars and to group together to keep house. The ships in the harbour are, in a great measure, deserted... Fortunate the family, whatever its position, which retains its servants at any sacrifice... Drained of its labouring population, the price of provisions in the towns is naturally on the increase.[3]

Ellen Clacy, who panned for gold beside her brother, recounted her experience on arriving in Melbourne in *A Lady's Visit to the Gold Diggings of Australia.*

> Our party, on returning to the ship the day after our arrival, witnessed the French leave-taking of all her crew, who during the absence of the captain, jumped overboard, and were quickly picked up and landed by various boats about. The desertion of the ships by the sailors is an every-day occurrence; the diggings themselves, or the large amount they could obtain for the run home from another master, offer too many temptations. Consequently, our passengers had the amusement of hauling up from the hold their different goods and chattels; and so great was the confusion, that fully a week elapsed before they were all got to shore.[4]

Others arrived to make their fortune with no intention of ever holding a shovel. Miners needed food, equipment and other amenities of life: 'Carters, carpenters, store men, wheelwrights, butchers, shoemakers etc, usually in the long run make a fortune quicker than the diggers themselves, and certainly with less hard work or risk of life.'[5] When British miner Henry Brown visited the diggings he often 'heard men, who have carried off honours at their colleges say, "Oh! If my father had but brought me up to anything useful, either baker, butcher or stonemason, what a fortune I would make."'

The cities emptied as men raced to the goldfields, in many cases leaving their women and children behind to fend for themselves. These 'California Widows' moved in together for protection and support and a tent city grew up in what would become South Melbourne, almost completely populated by women and children. Clacy, like many others, refused to be left behind and followed their men.

> Never shall I forget the scene, it well repaid a journey even of 16,000 miles. The trees had been all cut down; it looked like a sandy plain, or one vast unbroken succession of countless gravel pits – the earth was everywhere turned up – men's heads in every direction were popping up and down from their holes ... The rattle of the cradle, as it swayed to and fro, the sounds of the pick and the shovel, the busy hum of so many thousands, the innumerable tents, the stores with large flags hoisted above them, flags of every shape, colour, and nation, from the lion and the unicorn of England to the Russian eagle, the strange

yet picturesque costume of the diggers themselves, all contributed to render the scene novel in the extreme.[6]

It was not only the lure of gold that brought men and women halfway around the world, but in the case of those from Britain an opportunity to break free of the class system.

> They have no masters. They go wherever they please and work when they will. Healthy exercise, delightful scenery, and clear and buoyant atmosphere maintain an excitement of the spirits and a glow of animal enjoyment peculiar to bush life. It is not what you were, but what you are that is the criterion; and although your father might have been my Lord of England all over, it goes for nothing in this equalising colony of gold and beef and mutton. Work is the word; and if you cannot do this, you are no use there.[7]

By 1861, about 100,000 men were working on the goldfields but the days of the individual miner were numbered as the surface gold, up to 40 feet deep, was increasingly difficult to find. Bendigo, Ballarat, Castlemaine, Maryborough and Clunes were on their way to becoming company towns as crushing mills were built to extract the gold from quartz-bearing rock. Diggers were outraged at this competition, machinery was sabotaged and plants burnt. It was inevitable that with the first glorious rush over, men were leaving the goldfields. The disappointment of many was tangible.

> We have seen sufficient already to show the falsity of the Arabian Nights' fables, which the Melbournians have circulated all over the world. The idea of walking up to Mount Alexander in a couple of days, and shovelling up a few sack-bags full of gold, and going home again, is very charming, and quite as true as the romance of Aladdin's lamp. The history of this, our memorable journey to the goldfields, will show what a gigantic undertaking going on to the diggings really is. And our history is but that of thousands. We are not the only ones who have had hardship, accidents, and sickness to encounter. Hundreds have already gone back again, cursing those who sent such one-sided statements of the goldfields and of the climate.[8]

Many, indeed, felt that a great deal of the publicity about the glories of the goldfields had simply been to populate the new country.

Coping with all this gold – dust, nuggets and chips – in the swags of independent miners, and the larger quantities from the crushing mills, was a tremendous challenge for the young country. British and American banks employed gold buyers to set up shop on the diggings and buy gold from the diggers, which was then transported to Melbourne. In this country with a very high population of ex-convicts, security was of great concern. The banks had the facilities for mounting guards, but not so the individual digger and many lost everything to bushrangers.

As early as 1861 the Melbourne mint had run out of room and a treasury was built. Once the gold reached the mint, it was struck into tokens with a value of £1, £2, £4 and £8, with the standard value of £4 per ounce of gold. However, things did not remain so simple and straightforward. American banks began to buy into gold and Britain was afraid that it would lose control over the Australian money interest. To head off the Americans, the British decided to establish a branch of the Royal Mint in Australia. Melbourne, Sydney and Adelaide fought each other for the privilege and it was finally awarded to Sydney, which began striking sovereigns in 1853. These sovereigns had exactly the same weight as those of their English counterparts; the dies were made in London, but had a unique design. (The last sovereign was struck in 1932.) Victoria and South Australia, not at all happy about the official location of the mint, began to mint their own coins. This currency failed as it had no legal status and the Sydney coinage became official imperial legal tender in 1857; by 1868, South Australia followed suit. It was not until 1872 that Victoria set up a Melbourne branch of the Royal Mint.

These facts are vitally important when considering what quantity of gold might have been on board the *General Grant* in 1866.

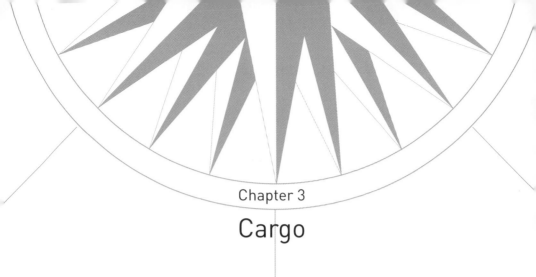

Chapter 3

Cargo

At this early stage of her career, the *General Grant* was not much more than what we might call a tramp. There are no records to indicate that she was to follow any particular itinerary, or that regular runs from Boston to Australia were ever to be part of her future. As a part-owner, Captain Loughlin was in a stronger position than most captains to arrange consignment cargo. On arriving in Melbourne, he had only two weeks to refit the ship, find new crew members, oversee the inevitable repairs necessary after the long ocean voyage and fill his ship with paying cargo for a voyage to London. Why was this her destination? Had there been previous arrangements for a cargo far more valuable than the usual hides and wool? This is the central mystery of the *General Grant*.

There is a record of the ship's manifest. In the hold were items typical of the cargo of an outgoing ship of the time, with one exception – two boxes of gold. There has been much speculation, however, that she was carrying much more gold than this.

2057 bales of wool	753 calfskins
136 packages leather	18 bales woollens
1281 packages bark	26 bales skins
130 packages pelts	87 bales rags
10,446 horns	4146 hides
720 pounds Myall wood	170 packages sundries
1 quantity bone, hoof	2 boxes gold – 2576 ounces
1 bundle hides	and 6 dwt [pennyweight]

The manifest gold would have had a value of about $US77,000 (about $US1,803,200 today, based on the rate of $US700 per ounce for gold). As valuable as that may seem, it does not compare to the great treasure ships of history, and nor is it a rich enough prize to have enticed so many men into the dangerous waters of the subantarctic.

Over the years, the perceived value of the *General Grant's* cargo has soared to astronomical heights. Fact – there were two boxes of gold aboard. Fact – a number of the passengers were returning miners who were carrying their own gold with them. Fact – the ship was carrying ballast, including 9 tons of spelter (impure zinc). Now we move into the realm of speculation. Unsubstantiated reports mention sums of £400,300 gold sovereigns and £18,000 carried by individuals. The manifest shows that 170 sundry packages were placed in the captain's safe but some say that many passengers preferred to guard their gold themselves.

As to why the *General Grant* was bound for London, the answer may lie in an item of news that arrived in Melbourne shortly before she docked. 'Intelligence reached Falmouth yesterday that the fine Australian passenger vessel, the "London", foundered at sea on Thursday last, and that of her crew and passengers, 289 all told, the only survivors, nineteen in number, had landed at the westernmost Channel port.' The *London* had left Gravesend on 30 December, under the command of Captain Martin, and struck such bad weather in the Channel that she had to shelter at Spithead. At Plymouth on 4 January, she had 'embarked a large number of passengers, an unusually large proportion of whom were old colonists returning to Australia'. With the crew, this gave the *London* a complement of 289 souls. The next day she encountered 'very heavy weather, with rain; boisterous and unsettled weather continuing on the 8th. This increased next day to a gale, during which a series of minor disasters befell her. It was then, at ten o'clock on the morning of that fatal Thursday, that Captain Martin had the terrible task of making known to the 200 passengers that the ship was sinking, and they must prepare for the worst'.[1]

Apart from the tragic loss of life, the disaster had far-reaching consequences. The *London* had a regular schedule so much of her cargo space for the return journey had been spoken for. Brokers immediately began the search for replacement vessels to take cargo to England. Without a doubt, some of it ended up on the *General Grant*, but no one knows if it included a consignment from the Bank of New South Wales en route to the Bank of England.

The first significant delivery of gold to the Bank of England seems to have been from Sydney on 17 January 1852. In 2000, G.P. Dyer, the librarian and curator at the Royal Mint in London explained that by 1866 the Royal Mint had a branch in Sydney 'specifically to convert locally found gold into coin. However, nearly all the gold bullion that came to the Royal Mint at that time reached the Mint directly from the Bank of England and, after coining into half-sovereigns and sovereigns, was returned to the Bank.'[2]

If, and it is a big if, the Bank of New South Wales was shipping gold bars to England, they would surely have entrusted it to the relatively unknown *General Grant* only because she was the only suitable ship available: she was, at least, licensed to carry United States mail and was equipped with a large safe. Another possibility is that Captain Loughlin, on hearing of this valuable cargo, decided to seize this opportunity to go to London rather than directly back to Boston. Another possibility, however, is that the gold, if it was aboard, could have been destined for any one of the independent gold brokers, who might have been less particular about their choice of ship.

An intriguing reference has only relatively recently come to light. A short piece from an unidentified newspaper datelined 'Brisbane 13/6/50' noted that :

'A Sydney Business man, H. Marfleet, possesses notes written by Wm. Sanguilly who was the last man to leave the wreck (of the *General Grant*), and who was in charge of the cargo. Under the captain's instructions Sanguilly had a special consignment marked as spelter to deceive certain ex-convicts and possible pirates among the crew and passengers.'

In 1952 the same Harry Marfleet, a 'dealer in stocks and shares, also warehouse employee', submitted a play to the Register of Copyrights for the Commonwealth of Australia. The application was originally for a 'dramatic work', but this was struck out and 'literary work' substituted by another hand. Marfleet had spent 10 years writing a play called *The Drama of the General Grant*.

On 26 December 1970 the Melbourne *Herald* reported that a five-page outline of a play amateurishly written and typed had recently been discovered in the archives of the Commonwealth of Australia Copyright Office and had therefore been unavailable to those searching for the *General Grant's* gold until now. The article repeated the claim that Marfleet had been in possession of notes written by William Sanguilly and that he had based his play outline on these.

The play's outline has Captain Loughlin befriending an orphaned William Sanguilly and promoting him to supervise cargo, then having him secretly remove additional boxes of gold from underneath his cabin floor to a secret hiding place. It seems most unlikely that an 18-year-old able seaman would hold this responsibility, but the piece makes for fascinating reading.

[The captain] sees young Will sitting on a hatch, looking very downcast. The little captain lifts up Will's chin and says, 'You won't leave me lad. I need you now for my right hand man remember! This is where your schooling comes in handy.' He takes Will to his cabin, hands him the cargo lists and says, 'I promote you to super cargo man in port. We are taking passengers and a valuable cargo of gold intended for the steamer s.s. *London*. She sank in the Bay of Biscay on her voyage to this country. You see nine tons of spelter that is gold in disguise. The shipping agents, you and myself only know of this for fear of mutiny or pirates on the high seas.'

At sea, Captain Loughlin goes one night to Will's bunk, shakes the lad. 'I want you to help me move the gold. I fear we may have trouble.' Gently, puts his forefinger to his mouth and whispers, 'Come to my cabin in a few minutes lad.' Will arrives. 'Shut the door, Will,' says Captain.

'I do not know my crew or passengers, or we may meet pirates before we reach London. I want you to swear with this Bible in your hand that what we do this night, you will tell no man.' The Captain then lifts a trap door in the floor of his cabin, goes down the small ladder with his lantern. Will follows. They are now in the ship's storeroom, where, also is stacked, the boxes of gold. Captain opens a heavy door in the bulk head – through this door they go with the lantern. 'Now Will, help me move these pieces of timber to make a hole big enough in which to put the gold.' They carry the boxes of gold in and put them in the hole. Now they put the timber back on top. The gold is now well hidden.'[3]

It would certainly have been safer to move gold in the quiet of night but it is unlikely that such a thing could have been kept a secret for so many years.

A totally different theory holds that the gold never left Australia and that the *General Grant* was deliberately wrecked to hide the theft. There is absolutely no proof that there was more gold aboard than stated on the manifest. Despite the usual care of financial institutions to keep careful track of all transactions, the documents from the bank have been lost – or destroyed. Stranger things have happened, so let us consider the option that there *was* unreported gold on board. Three major considerations may have led to the secrecy: fear of pirates; fear of mutiny and theft on the high seas; and avoidance of taxes and export duties.

The avoidance of tax is unlikely to have applied to a commercial shipment, such as that of the bank. It was very different for the individual. Victoria abolished the gold licence fee in 1855, and New South Wales followed suit two years later, replacing it with a gold export tax of 2s 6d per ounce minus a miner's right of £1 per annum.

Most writers have given no credence to the threat of pirates as a reason to hide the presence of the gold. The latter had, however, been a significant enough menace that in 1861 the United States government sent the Pacific Fleet – six small ships carrying 100 guns all told – to patrol the area from San Francisco to Panama, north to Alaska and south to Chile. Their mandate was to protect the whaling fleets around Hawaii and guard the waters of China and Japan, Australia and the southern seas from maritime marauders, although the primary danger at this time was from Confederate raiders, rather than from conventional pirates.

During the two years before Captain Loughlin left San Francisco, two hijack plots had been uncovered. The most dramatic was the exposure of a Captain Law, who at one time had worked for the Pacific Mail Steamship Company. He bought and armed the *J.M. Chapman*, a 90-ton schooner, and with 16 men planned to go to Guadeloupe, hoist the Confederate flag and attack vessels of the North. This could in part have been Civil War strategy, but their plans extended to capturing a Pacific Mail steamer and then continuing to the China Sea and the Indian Ocean. Another plot to capture California-bound ships was discovered in the spring of 1864. After this revelation every passenger and all baggage was searched and any passenger with a gun was required to surrender it to the captain for the duration of the voyage.

Shortly before the *General Grant* left San Francisco on her voyage to India via Singapore, the *Sea King*, flying the British flag, had sailed from London. When she reached Pacific waters, she raised the Confederate flag and sailed as a privateer, destroying over a million dollars' worth of shipping before returning to England at the end of the war. In 1865, four more ships were added to the United States Pacific fleet, bringing the number to 11, and another six were added in 1866.[4] Captain Loughlin would have been aware of these events and it would be reasonable for him to take extra precautions if carrying a cargo of gold. Even the quantity of gold listed on the manifest would have been a worthwhile prize for a mutinous crew or an attack by lucky pirates.

The risk of piracy, at least in the traditional sense, can, however, be overstated. Eunson states quite categorically that 'piracy was unknown in the Australian trade'.[5] Sailing vessels, as a rule, carried a certain amount of permanent ballast in the form of pig iron known as kentledge. Ballast is usually defined as non-paying weight which was carried to make a ship seaworthy, the amount depending on the cargo. But the term can also be used to refer to heavy cargo carried in a lower hold to provide stability. In this case, the shipper would pay a significantly reduced rate on the goods. The *General Grant* was said to have been carrying, as part of her ballast, nine tons of zinc residue from smelting – the famous spelter. This would seem a reasonable choice for ballast since, being a loose material, it would allow the ship to flex. Using a builder's rule of thumb for calculating ballast – tonnage divided by eight and the result divided by five, then subtract the two quotients[6] – the 1103-ton *General Grant* should have been carrying 110 tons of ballast. The builder's records no longer exist to tell us how much permanent ballast was placed on the ship, so it is difficult to say what proportion nine tons would have been of the variable weight ballast. If it had been nine tons (288,000 ounces) of gold rather than spelter, it would be worth $US201,160,000 on today's market (calculated at $US700 per ounce). An enticing prize to be sure.

It seems a very straightforward matter to eliminate spelter as the ballast. A 1902 New Zealand government memo stated unequivocally that the ballast could not have been spelter since 'there were no smelting works in Australia at that time and no zinc, tin or lead smelted together'.[7] Indeed, zinc was not discovered in Australia until 1882. It is not impossible, however, that the *General Grant* was light on ballast and took on board spelter that had been offloaded from another fully ballasted vessel.

Recent research by one of the treasure hunting syndicates has found that a number of vessels at this time were indeed carrying spelter as ballast. It came mostly from China and was carried to London as a useful form of ballast. As Eunson notes, in 1864 the *Omar Pashar* carried, along with wool, hides and casks of tallow, 4000 ounces of gold and 20 tons of spelter which, together with stones, made up a ballast estimated at

430 tons.[8] The 1902 memo considers that other gold may have been aboard and refers to Captain N. C. Sorensen, who later mounted a search expedition and believed that there was a great deal more gold on board.

> He gets his belief from a Mr. White, supposed to be living in Sydney, Australia, whose partner was lost with about $2,000,000 he was taking home. Also he, Captain Sorensen, claimed to have interviewed a man who helped store the gold away in strong boxes under the Captain's cabin and who himself lost considerable money.
>
> The German, Captain Sorensen speaks about, was a Miner in Ballarat. He went home in the *General Grant* as a sailor and was rescued. In 1878, this man had worked for Captain Sorensen. Says he had £18,000 in the vessel himself and saw between 100 and 200 boxes of gold stored on board the vessel. Captain knew him by the name of Fred.[9]

The surviving *General Grant* crew members were William Ferguson, Cornelius Drew, Joseph Jewell, William Sanguilly and Aaron Hayman. The only possible individual who might have been identified as 'German' by his name would have been Aaron Hayman, who was returning to England after visiting his brother. The difficulty with this theory is that Hayman, born in Devon, would have spoken with a strong regional accent. He had been so shattered by the experience that he settled in Australia, vowing never to set foot on a ship again. His family had been miners in Britain so he could very easily have been a miner in Ballarat. It is conceivable, considering that Aaron was an unusual name, that he used another name outside the home, so he may have been the mysterious Fred. It is unlikely that, as a visitor, he would have had £18,000 with him, unless he was taking money home for his brother. On the other hand, if his brother had that much money, and entrusted it to Aaron, why was the latter working his way home as a seaman?

The American William Sanguilly is the seaman most commonly linked to the supposedly hidden gold but, at the time of departure, he was only 18. As the government memo mused, 'The great question is whether sailing ships carried gold at all in 1866 and if they did whether any such sum as $15,000,000 which the Captain claims was on board, could possibly have been on board one ship.'[10] It was feasible, as was evidenced when the United States Mail steamship *Central America* was found in 1988. Returning from the California goldfields, she sank in a hurricane off the coast of the Carolinas in 1857 with the loss of

425 lives. Modern science, technology and an investment of $US10 million culminated in the raising of a fabulous treasure including gold ingots, nuggets and coins from a depth of 8000 feet. The largest gold bar, christened the Eureka, weighed 933 ounces and was stamped with an 1857 currency value of $17,433.57. Appendix I shows estimates of the amount of gold carried on the *General Grant*.

One intriguing fact perhaps tilts the scales towards the belief that there may have something very unusual about the *General Grant*'s cargo. Her builders made a tidy profit of almost 60 per cent when they sold her. Before she left Melbourne, the owners insured her with the Tasmanian and Launceston Insurance Company for £165,000 ($US1,102,200). She had cost £8,141 ($US81,167) to build in 1864,[11] and was sold for £14,070 ($US94,900) in 1866. Even supposing her cargo was worth, at a conservative estimate, £28,000 ($US192,600), the total value of the ship and cargo would be in the vicinity of £42,000, so why would she be insured for almost four times her value?

To put things in perspective, insurance premiums for ships and cargoes in the days of sail were so high that owners usually underinsured. Errors in transcription are always possible, but taking the information at face value and when one considers the premiums that had to be paid, it is possible to conclude that the owners were covering something very valuable indeed. In 1994 the *Sea Search* group, working backwards with currency and gold values, reached the conclusion that *if* it was gold that was being insured for this amount, the consignment would have been an astronomical 22,000 ounces, worth over $US11,000,000 in 1994.[12] No wonder treasure hunters still dream of the Auckland Islands.

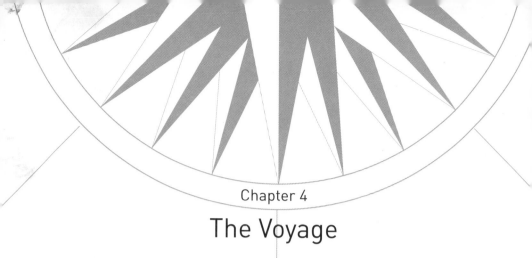

Chapter 4

The Voyage

Since 1852, tens of thousands of dreamers had been drawn to Melbourne. Far from being a dowdy colonial outpost, the city had grown into the 'Paris of the Antipodes'. Those who were to travel to London on the *General Grant* would have had no difficulty finding accommodation, for the city abounded with hotels. They would have had their choice of the Port Phillip Club Hotel, with its arcaded upper storeys and broad frontage, the Clarence Hotel, the old Criterion Hotel on Collins Street or any number of less pricey establishments. As they strolled along Swanson or Elizabeth Streets, those who had been in the backcountry for some years would have been overwhelmed by the vibrant life of the city, the shops and the hustle and bustle. As Ellen Clacy wrote,

> all nations, classes and costumes are represented there. Chinamen, with pigtails and loose trowsers [*sic*]; Aborigines with a solitary blanket flung over them; Vandemonian pickpockets, with cunning eyes and light fingers – all, in truth, from the successful digger in his blue serge shirt, and with green veil still hanging round his wide-awake [a type of bush hat], to the fashionably-attired, newly-arrived 'Gent' from London, who stares around him in amazement and disgust.[1]

The passengers' days were filled with sightseeing, final shopping and organisation. Finally, on the morning of 4 May 1866, they would have made their way to the station, paid their sixpence and boarded Melbourne and Hobson's Bay Railway for the 2½-mile trip to the port of Sandridge, on Hobson's Bay.

They were a mixed lot – families, professional men and miners, shopkeepers and craftsmen. Of the 56 passengers, 26 appear to have been single men or married men without children, five men were sailing with their wives and/or children and three women were travelling with their children but not their husbands. Only five passengers were aged 40 or over. Fifteen men, women and children occupied cabins; there were 41 in steerage, that area 'between decks', immediately below the main deck. Conditions for passengers had improved over the last few years, beginning in 1842 with a law ensuring that each steerage passenger had at least 10 square feet of personal space, but those travelling in this part of the ship had no illusions about what awaited them: a number had made the trip out to Australia so had already experienced the uncertainty of a crowded, noisy, foul-smelling and uncomfortable journey that would tax everyone's patience and understanding. The challenge of coping with young children in such an open area with lack of privacy would be daunting. The moment all the passengers set foot on the *General Grant*, their lives were in the hands of Captain Loughlin. He had the legal power to marry and bury and, they hoped, the skill to take them safely to their destination.

Loughlin and his crew of 24 men and two women had been busy in the days leading up to the voyage. While his officers negotiated with the salesmen in the chandler's yards to get the best price for new ropes and canvas to replace worn items from the long trip around the Cape of Good Hope, Loughlin cast about for cargo for the return trip. Seamen spent time below decks, readying accommodation, loading stores and water and doing a thousand and one jobs in preparation for the three-month voyage.

On 5 May the moment of departure came: shouted orders, seamen scrambling aloft to set the sails, hawsers cast on board for the last time, farewells shouted across the widening space between the quay and the passengers lining the rails taking in their last view of Port Phillip. To their right, they could see long ridges of sand stretching towards the east and, on the other side, rugged, rocky cliffs topped by a lighthouse, some pilots' cottages and a few wind-tortured trees.

The records pertaining to those aboard show a number of discrepancies (see Appendix II). The bride of first officer Bartholomew Brown was travelling with her husband but the only other Brown recorded is a N. Brown, listed as crew, not as a passenger. Mary Ann Jewell, the wife of the seaman Joseph, is shown as crew, later identified as stewardess, but was, by her own statement, a fare-paying passenger. In both cases it is assumed that the women were signed on as crew so as to be able to travel together with their husbands. The ages of the children must be taken with a grain of salt. A child under two was considered an infant, and thus would travel free; other fare divisions, depending on the ship or company, would be one to seven and eight to 13; over 13 was counted as an adult. A certain amount of deception was common to save money on fares.

The passenger list raises many questions that can never be answered. Why, for example, was Elizabeth Oat travelling alone with her young family? Mary, the eldest was just six, Rosella was four, Ada, three and Elizabeth, one. Did her husband plan to join her in England or had his life ended in the new land so that she was forced to return to her family? The only other child in cabin accommodation was baby Emilia Morinini and her 25-year-old father Alessandro. What tragedy lay behind his setting out with an infant? The Rays, a young couple without children, were also able to afford to travel as cabin passengers. Nineteen-year-old John Woodrow could also afford this relative luxury, perhaps because he was the son of a wealthy family. Befitting his position, Marist priest Father Paul Sarda also travelled comfortably. The other cabin passengers listed were J. Edel, William Deans, John Tebbutt (or Tebutt) and F. Johnstone. Although listed on the passenger list as Mr F. Johnstone, according to the *Daily Southern Cross* of 13 March 1867, he was in fact Lieutenant-Colonel Frederick Johnstone of Raglan and late of the Bengal Army.

The Lansons, a French farming family – Auguste and Clemeace and their children George (20), Emily (11), Clemeace (three) and Arthur (one) – were crowded together. Elizabeth Roberts, travelling on her own, would have had her hands full with Francis (three), Ann (two) and John (eight months). Caroline Smith was another 'single mother' travelling with Elizabeth (seven) and William (five). Nicholas and Rose Allen organised their family of Mary (eight), Margaret (three) and Josephine (11 months). Francis and Sarah Oldfield, no doubt worried about their active pair, 11-year-old Frederick and 10-year-old Ernest, getting into mischief during the long, boring trip.

The single men in steerage – David Ashworth (30), James Barry (31), James Bayles (28), Patrick Caughey (34), William Frost (40), Matthew Hamilton (30), John Harvey (28), Richard Jefferies (42), P. Kelly (32), H. Kent (25), K. Krentz (25), W. Main (28), A. Mitchell (28), Charles Newman (32), William Stevenson (34), James Teer (34), Samuel Templeton (35) and P. Wise (25) – had only their situation in common. David Ashworth was a young businessman. Patrick Caughey and James Teer were old friends from the same village in Ireland who had met again on the West Coast goldfields. Teer, who was born in 1826 or 1827, had left Ireland at the age of 18 and spent 20 years in Australia and New Zealand working as a miner and a mariner. He had won some fame on the West Coast in December 1864 for piloting the first storekeeper's provisions across the Hokitika Bar in the SS *Nelson*. He had returned to Australia in 1865 and was now bound for Ireland with his savings.

There has always been some speculation as to the number of miners on board the *General Grant* who were perhaps taking their gold back to England. A careful analysis of the passenger list shows the following passengers appear to be listed as miners: William Stevenson, Richard Jefferies, Matthew Hamilton, John Harvey, Nicholas Allen, William Frost, H. Kent, W. Main, A. Mitchell, P. Kelly, P. Wise, James Teer, Patrick Caughey, Samuel Templeton, Charles Newman, Thomas Batchelor, David Ashworth and K. Krentz. At least four passengers in cabin class could also have been miners.

As Australia faded into the distance, and the ship met the swells of the open ocean, the passengers became aware of the ever-changing sea. Grey-aquamarine spume flew from the bow; waves captured and refracted the light into myriad shades of grey, green and blue. The sky went on forever, or was blocked by the next wave as the ship sank into a trough. Cape pigeons, the little spitfires of the sea, streaked above, while albatrosses soared in the leaden heavens. The ocean was all-encompassing.

The sound of the sea aboard a ship is very different from the sound of waves lapping on a shingled shore, or crashing into a storm-etched cliff. Everything on a ship reflects the sound of the sea – the resonance in the hull, the ruffle in the sails, the clinking of rigging, the miscellaneous squeaks below deck. The smell that a landlubber associates with the sea is totally absent: the odour of rotting seaweed, fish and wet sand belongs only to that tiny area where the sea meets the land. Far from land, the smell is almost an absence, indescribable and clean, in the same way that the sound of a northern forest in winter can only be described as the lack of sound.

The weather for the first six days was relatively pleasant, with clear late autumn temperatures and fair winds. Despite this, there was the tension that always exists at sea, no matter how smooth and uneventful the voyage to the moment. It is not fear but awareness. It is the constant physical demand of always having to know how and where you are going to place your feet and your body before you move; looking around you to check what handhold is within reach. This is no place for bravado – the seaman's credo of 'one hand for myself and one hand for the ship' is not to be taken lightly.

As the passengers settled in and became familiar with the routine of shipboard life they formed friendships they hoped would sustain them on the long voyage. We can imagine Elizabeth Oat perhaps helping Alessandro Morinini with wee Emilia. To find other women with young children she would have had to turn to the steerage class passengers. It is easy to visualise the Oldfield boys racing around the ship, getting underfoot; or perhaps they were overawed by the whole experience and kept close to their parents.

As the days passed, those who had been laid low by the misery of seasickness began to find their sea legs and appreciate returning appetite. Routines developed and sleep came more easily as they accustomed themselves to the tiny bunks and the roll of the ship. The regular creaks and groans of the vessel and the sound of the waves against the hull had become part of the normal world – remarkable only when the tone changed. Anyone who had woken during the night of 10–11 May would have felt a distinct change in the movement of the ship, though not enough to be disturbing. Topside, the officer on watch logged the barometer reading, noting a steady drop over the last few hours. With the dawn came dark clouds on the horizon.

The great, apparently empty expanse of the southern ocean is deceptive, for rising from the ocean bed are scattered rocks and islands waiting to snare unwary ships. With 1200 miles under the keel, the officers knew that they were coming within range of the Snares (100 miles south of New Zealand's Bluff) and Auckland Islands; only when these were left safely behind could they confidently set their course across the broad Pacific towards the Horn.

Even if they had been able to take regular and accurate sightings, there was always the question of the accuracy of the charts. They simply had to trust that their charts were correct, though this was unwise given that some charts of that area had been deliberately falsified earlier in the century to protect the location of rich sealing areas.

Sunrise at that latitude was at 7.46 am on 11 May. Captain Loughlin removed the sextant from its lined wooden box, 'shot' the sun, and recorded their position on the chart and in the ship's log. The dark clouds on the horizon soon rolled in and from this point on they would have to sail by dead reckoning. This was not the place to have to depend on an estimated position roughly calculated by advancing this last known position, using course, speed, time and distance travelled. Trusting that

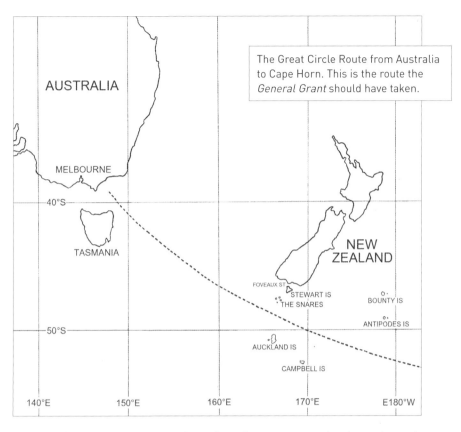

AUSTRALIA

The Great Circle Route from Australia to Cape Horn. This is the route the *General Grant* should have taken.

MELBOURNE

40°S

TASMANIA

NEW ZEALAND

FOVEAUX ST
STEWART IS
THE SNARES
BOUNTY IS
ANTIPODES IS

50°S

AUCKLAND IS

CAMPBELL IS

140°E   150°E   160°E   170°E   E180°W

the calculations were correct, they plotted a course to take them through the 155-nautical-mile gap between the Snares and the Aucklands. The distance may seem great enough, but unseen and unfelt currents could pull the unwary mariner southward. Tides were well understood by seamen, but the existence of these deep ocean currents running like fearsome rivers within the sea were still very much of a mystery. Captains came to know the peculiarities of the seas they sailed regularly, but William Loughlin was far from home.

During the next two days of fog and cloud, the *General Grant* ploughed steadily towards the Auckland Islands 'before half a gale of wind'[2] from the north-west with a heavy sea running. Captain Loughlin doubled the lookouts. Passengers and crew peered into the swirling mist as the tension grew. Those passengers not braving the damp wind on deck remained below talking in uneasy groups, or keeping their own counsel in their bunks.

On the night of the 13 May 1866, in a light wind and slightly choppy seas, the nightmare began.

Chapter 5

Disaster

Slowly, the unseen current pulled the ship southward as the sails reached out for the light north-west wind. Joseph Jewell remembered the night being black with a cold rain falling, the dense clouds hiding the full moon. At half past ten came the dreaded cry: 'Land on the port bow!' The helmsman, William Ferguson, threw the wheel hard to port. (The helm on a vessel like the *General Grant* was constructed in such a way that turning the wheel to port would swing the ship to starboard.)

The resting watch raced topside where, even in the pitch darkness, each man could lay his hands on the belaying pin securing the rope he needed to square away the yards. Gradually she wore around, onto a south by east course that was held for about half an hour before Captain Loughlin ordered an easterly heading. He had fallen into the same trap as Captain George Dalgarno of the ill-fated *Invercauld*, almost exactly two years before in exactly the same place. The land sighted was not the main Auckland Island, but Disappointment Island, lying off the west coast.

Twenty minutes after the course change land appeared again right ahead – 'like a cloud right over our heads', as Jewell later described it. He went on to make a very interesting observation: 'The vessel was then brought to the wind on the port tack, but being a bad sailor and lightly laden, she made more lee than headway against such a heavy sea.'[1] This confirmed earlier stories that the *General Grant* had its design problems, but lightly laden? Other witnesses said that there was a 'slight swell' or a 'dead calm'.[2] We now enter a realm of conflicting eyewitness reports which, considering the length of time before the stories were told to the outside world and the trauma the survivors had undergone, is not really surprising. James Teer said that 'the land had the appearance of a fog bank and it was on our lee beam, about three or four miles distant'.[3] Was this really possible on a dark, rainy night, or had the moon broken through so that he experienced the phenomenon of seeing above the mist? Mist at sea can appear, disappear and reappear in a matter of minutes. It can hug the sea, completely blocking visibility ahead while everything above can be seen clearly.

Teer did not mention any cliffs, so it may have been that Jewell was looking in exactly the right direction at the moment the mist cleared slightly. He may not have thought of pointing it out, assuming that the lookouts had seen what he had seen. If he *was* the only person who saw the cliffs at this moment, and had he acted earlier, the outcome might have been very different.

The die was now cast, for the wind had dropped to almost a dead calm and the ship was next to unmanageable. Captain Loughlin used all his considerable skill to trap any breath of wind in the massive sails but with each rise and fall of the heavy south-west swell the ship edged closer to what Teer called the 'fatal rocks'. Jewell set the time of the first contact with the rocks just past midnight, Teer placed it an hour later, but 60 minutes here or there did not alleviate the terror. The bow struck a rock, the jib boom was carried away, the force pushed the ship backwards against the other point that formed a small bay, and the spanker boom and rudder were broken off. The violent shock against the rudder caused the wheel to spin and Ferguson broke several ribs.

Thousands of words have been written on what befell the *General Grant* that night, actions have been glorified, the situation described in purple Victorian prose, but who better to pick up the tale than Jewell in a letter to his parents?

The vessel then turned with her head to the east and went into a cave that was about 100 yards from shore. She struck the second time. When the foremast struck the roof of the cave, it went close to the deck, the main topmast and mizzen-top-gallant mast were carried away with it. Everybody got into the cabin out of the way of the falling spars and large stones which were falling from the roof of the cave. And such a night of horror I think was never experienced by human beings as we passed in the cave for seven long hours. It was so dark that you could not see your fingers before your eyes, and there we were with falling spars and large stones tumbling from the roof of the cave (some of which went through the deck), and so we remained until daylight. The sides of the cave were perpendicular, with the exception of a ledge of rocks that projected under the starboard quarter of the vessel, where she kept bumping heavily during the night, and we were afraid she would sink before morning, and if she had there would not be anyone left to tell the tale.[4]

During that long night, the passengers gathered together precious belongings and men begged the captain for their valuables from the safe. The crew leaned over the rails with lanterns, trying to make sense of their surroundings. 'We could see then the overhanging rocks, and no place where a bird could rest upon them.'[5]

The ship lay quietly with 25 fathoms (150 feet) under her stern. The ship slowly ground her way into the cave. Now Captain Loughlin made another critical decision that may have led to a much higher death toll. He balanced the dangers of trying to evacuate the ship in the dark with rocks and rigging falling onto the deck, against waiting for daylight, and chose the latter. Unfortunately, by daylight the wind had risen.

There they waited, surrounded by a cacophony of sound, echoing and re-echoing from the cavern walls and roof: the crack of breaking stays, the crashes as the masts fell, the dull thud and splintering of timber as rocks and boulders went through the deck, the shouts and cries of the seamen. Terrified children clung to their mothers as they dressed them for the escape they prayed would be theirs. Reports suggest that Father Sarda was equal to the challenge of giving strength to others as he faced his own death. He moved gently and comfortingly from group to group, praying with them and finding the right words to bring calm and hope. Bartholomew Brown and Joseph Jewell were torn between their duties to the ship and concern for the safety of their wives.

As the blackness of night was finally replaced by the grey light of dawn the terror-stricken passengers and crew were at last able to see the total hopelessness of their situation. The wreckage strewn everywhere, and the great holes in the deck where rocks had crashed through, made movement difficult. The constant grinding of the ship on the ledge and the sides of the cave and the booming of the waves surging through their prison magnified their fear. As the vessel continued to work her way into the cave, the stump of the main mast was pushed through the hull and the *General Grant* began to settle.

The crew was now able to see to cut away ropes and broken rigging and open places along the rail where the boats could be launched. The *General Grant* carried two 22-foot quarter-boats and a larger long boat with a 30-foot keel. Three able seamen, Peter McNevin, Andrew Morrison and David McClelland, were commanded to take one boat and try to find a place nearby where it would be possible to put rescued passengers ashore; they should then come back and report. The ship was settling rapidly: by the time the second boat was packed with supplies, 'a quantity of beef and pork and about fifty tins of bouilli' (meat ranging from pot roast to stewed whole chicken with vegetables), the main deck was level with the water and the sea was washing over the stern. First Officer Brown took Teer, Scott and Drew into the second boat to ferry women and children out to the first. The passengers were in a state of panic. Joseph Jewell tied his wife to a rope and she jumped into the water.

> Mr. Tier [*sic*] was in the boat and got hold of her, and if it had been possible to have got her into the boat I should have slung some of the other females the same way, but the boat was filling fast with the backwash from the sides of the cave, and it was as much as the men could do to keep her off the rocks. When I saw Tier pulling my wife's clothes off trying to get her into the boat, and could not do it, I jumped overboard and got her in myself. Two others [i.e. Patrick Caughey and Nicholas Allen] jumped after me and we all succeeded in getting in the boat; there were then nine persons in the boat and she half full of water. We pulled out to the first boat and put five of ours into her and were returning to the ship. When about 100 yards from her we saw the long boat float from off the vessel's stern with about forty persons in her. The boat could not get clear of the backwash from the rocks, and when about 30 yards from the ship she capsized and the vessel sank at the same time in 18 fathoms [108 feet] of water. We got as close to the long boat as possible, three [David Ashworth, Aaron Hayman and William Sanguilly] swam clear of the breakers and we picked them up; all was over with the others in a minute or two.[6]

Those in the other two lifeboats watched in horror as the hull of the ship sank below the waves. Bart Brown was frantic: his duties had taken him to safety while his wife remained on board. Screams echoed from the cliffs as those cast from the overturned boat struggled in the icy waves.

As Joseph Jewell explained,

One man was seen on the bottom of the boat and we made signals to the outer boat to save him, but prudence forbade them from rendering him any assistance, as the boat was so near the rocks, with the sea breaking heavily. When the mate wished again to return to the ship, we thought it useless, as we were unable to render assistance, and placed ourselves in great danger owing to the heavy sea and constant increase of wind.

While outside deliberating upon what was best to be done, I had an opportunity of seeing the whole of the cave. The rocks around it, I think, were about 400 feet high, and overhanging, The ship was underneath these about two lengths of herself. The coast, as far as we could see, was high, perpendicular rocks, and we saw no possibility of landing. We now consulted with each other, and with those in the other boat, upon what was best to be done. We concluded we could not assist those inside, as it was only endangering ourselves, owing to the constant increase of the sea and wind.

When we saw they were all gone we began to look for a landing place, but as far as the eye could reach, north or south, nothing could be seen but perpendicular cliffs.[7]

The anguish in those words 'we saw they were all gone' resonates through the years.

Jewell spared his parents some of the more heartrending details that other writers, like this one in the *Southland Times*, later described.

It is said that one of the survivors of the wreck had his wife and children on board, and that he left them on the poop crying to him for God's sake to save them in order to secure safety for himself. Horrible to relate still, he is said to have plucked from his wife's breast a gold brooch she wore just before he threw her from his knees, to which she had been clinging for succour in the hour of direst need.

Strong in contrast with this was the noble conduct of Mrs. Oat, who with her children got a seat in the boat that was capsized. When she was last seen she was struggling with the waves, with a child under each arm. The mate's wife was on board the ship, and he had arranged to return with the lifeboat, in which he was making a trip to the long boat, in order to bring her and the captain off. They were pulling close in to the wreck on their return, when the ship was seen settling down fast, and the men refused point blank to proceed further. The mate thus had to stand idly by and see the wife he had only just married fade from his sight forever, while he was powerless to help her.[8]

One woman and 14 men rowed away from the *General Grant*. Captain Loughlin was last seen standing on the cross-trees of his ship.

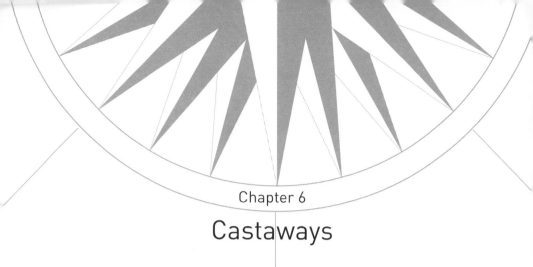

Chapter 6

Castaways

In the rising wind, shaken to their very heart's core, the survivors pulled towards Disappointment Island, eight miles to the north-west. Several times the tiny boats were almost swamped. Thwarted by the waves and current, they could not get back to the island and were forced to spend the night in the lee of a rocky islet, their faces turned against the driving rain and snow. With the grey dawn, they had been without food and water for 24 hours, but to survive they had to find the strength to row northwards to get around North Cape, which was protected by the fearsome Column Rocks. At least the wind and waves were not against them, but they had to set a course far enough to the west to avoid being swept onto the coastal rocks. They struggled all that day, but their goal was out of reach and they were forced once more to turn back to Disappointment Island. According to Jewell,

> In one of the boats, we had about fifty tins of soup and bouilli and about fifty pounds of pork. But misfortune still followed us, for in trying to get to land to get some water the boat swamped and we lost it all but nine tins of soup and three pounds of pork. The men got on the rocks and we got hold of their boat with ours and got her off the shore, and after a long while managed to get her bailed out and then backed our own boat as close as we could and threw a rope to the men and got them in their boat again.[1]

The wind shifted to the south-west and blew hard until midnight. When it slackened they started again for the north coast, finally turning east with the coast of the main island on their starboard. Resisting the temptation to row into the shelter of North Harbour, with its gentler slopes and beach, they pressed onwards towards Port Ross, where they hoped there

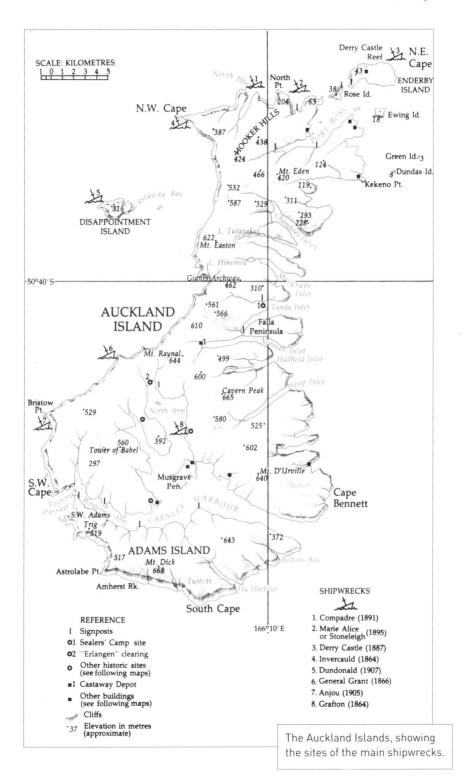

SCALE: KILOMETRES
1 0 1 2 3 4 5

Derry Castle
Reef ·3 N.E.
Cape
·3 ■
ENDERBY
ISLAND
38· Rose Id.
North Hbr.
·1 North
Pt. ·2
204 63
N.W. Cape
·4 18· Ewing Id.
·387 HOOKER HILLS PORT ROSS
·438
·424 ·124
·466 ·Mt. Eden Green Id.·3
420 8·Dundas Id.
·532 119· Kekeno Pt.
·587 ·329 ·311 Chambres Inlet
·293
228·
DISAPPOINTMENT ·316
ISLAND Castaway Bay L. Tutanekai
·5 622
·Mt. Easton
L. Hinemoa
·50°40'S Giants Archway 462
310· Grave
Inlet
·561 ·10 Tandu Inlet
·566
AUCKLAND Falla
ISLAND 610 Peninsula
Norman Inlet
■1 Hadfield Inlet
·6 Mt. Raynal ·499
644 Deep Inlet
2 ·600
O 525·
Bristow Cavern Peak
Pt. ·529 665
·7 ·580
North Arm ·8
·602
560 392
Tower of Babel ·Mt. D'Urville
297 640
Musgrave
S.W. Pen. Cape
Cape HARBOUR Bennett
Victoria CARNLEY
Passage Western Arm
S.W. Adams ·643 ·372
Trig
·519
ADAMS ISLAND Bollons Bay
517 Mt. Dick
Astrolabe Pt. 668
Amherst Rk. Turbott
Fly Harbour
South Cape 166°10'E

REFERENCE
I   Signposts
O1 Sealers' Camp site
O2 "Erlangen" clearing
o   Other historic sites
    (see following maps)
■1 Castaway Depot
■   Other buildings
    (see following maps)
    Cliffs
·37 Elevation in metres
    (approximate)

SHIPWRECKS

1. Compadre (1891)
2. Marie Alice
   or Stoneleigh (1895)
3. Derry Castle (1887)
4. Invercauld (1864)
5. Dundonald (1907)
6. General Grant (1866)
7. Anjou (1905)
8. Grafton (1864)

The Auckland Islands, showing
the sites of the main shipwrecks.

would be supplies and shelter. As another survivor remembered, 'We reached what appeared an entrance into a bay (very narrow), into which we steered. With the heavy sea running, and the rip, it was with much difficulty and danger effected. This is a narrow passage between the mainland and Rabbit Island (Rose Island) into Port Ross, but named by us "Welcome Bay".'[2] Jewell recorded that they spent three days in the boats, 'and wet through all the time, and bitter cold. My wife, through being cramped up so much, did not get the use of her limbs for months afterwards.'[3]

It is not clear from the descriptions exactly where they first landed. Port Ross is like a gigantic funnel, the flanges formed by a line from Enderby to Rose Islands to the north, and Ewing and Ocean Islands to the south; Laurie Harbour is the spout, reaching three miles inland between steep hills. The first level area along the eastern shore is in a small bay south of Lindley Point. There is no beach, but a maze of sea-worn black rocks and tidal pools. Mount Eden, with its pinnacle of volcanic outcrop, rises from the shore to the south-west. Barren scars of landslips point down the steep slopes. When you look upwards, the dense olearia and rata forest give way to a rugged, boggy area of poa grass; scattered across this area are sharp black cliffs. The view has not changed since John Baker, the surveyor, saw it in 1865: 'I found nothing but complete desolation, bleak and rugged mountains, without even much vegetation to cover their gaunt sides'.[4]

The islands had remained unknown to Europeans until Abraham Bristow, a captain for Enderby's South Sea Whale Fishing Company, first saw them through the mist in 1806 from his vessel *Ocean*. He did not have time to stop, but named them the Aucklands, after his father's friend, William Eden, Lord Auckland. He returned the next year in the *Sarah*, officially claimed them for Great Britain and named his anchorage Sarah's Bosom. Bristow's navigational and cartographic skills were remarkable; he placed the islands almost exactly and by 1823 they were to be found on Admiralty charts. This is a significant point, for one of the reasons given for so many wrecks on the Aucklands was that maps showed the islands at least 25 miles from their correct location. One account blamed this misconception directly on a statement by a crew member of the *General Grant*.

By 1840 the islands had become an important stopping-off place for subantarctic and Antarctic scientific expeditions. In 1849, Samuel Enderby, of the House of Enderby mentioned in *Moby Dick*, set out from England with three small ships to found the Hardwicke Settlement.

Taking with them pre-fabricated houses, skilled men and their families sailed for the Aucklands full of hopes and dreams for an independent life far from the rigid class system of England. This was to be *the* whaling settlement of the Southern Ocean, a transit point for whale oil destined for the hungry markets of Europe. Charles Enderby was a dreamer. He had managed to convince the Crown to grant him a lease for the whole island group and was appointed lieutenant governor. For the brief period from December 1849 to August 1852 the Auckland Islands held the same political status as Canada and the Australasian colonies of New South Wales, Victoria and New Zealand. However, Enderby was too late. The whales had been slaughtered almost to extinction and the poor soils, harsh climate and landscape doomed any dreams of successful faming. The settlers departed, leaving a silent graveyard on the hill, some cleared land, broken fences and the scattered detritus of their lives: an axe head here, a piece of tin there, a broken pot under a fallen log, nails from the buildings that had not been dismantled and taken back to New Zealand or Australia. These would become treasures to the desperate *General Grant* survivors.

Staggering with exhaustion, hypothermia and cramp, they fell onto the shore with barely enough strength to pull their boats clear of the greedy tide. They had reached the safety of land, but each of them knew that without food and warmth this safety was only an illusion.

In the panic of that awful night, no one thought to take survival gear beyond the tins of bouilli and some meat. There are two versions of the 'last match' story. In one, the first officer found one Lucifer match in his pocket; in the second he found a damp box in his pocket. The second version fits with Teer's account in the Wellington *Independent*: he said that Brown struck one match to see if it would light. It did, but 'as we had no dry brush or grass in readiness it was wasted'.[5] Brown frantically continued striking one match after the other: the next one failed, as did the next and the next. Teer became so angry at this thoughtless waste that he charged Brown, knocking him down. In the struggle he rescued the last precious match, which he placed in his hair to dry.

Brown's indiscriminate striking of the matches was just one indication that he, and probably most of his companions, were suffering from what is now known as post-traumatic stress disorder, which affects those

who have either directly experienced or witnessed, during or after the disaster, the loss of loved ones or friends, life threatening danger or physical harm (especially to children), exposure to gruesome death, bodily injury, or dead or maimed bodies, extreme environmental or human violence or destruction, intense emotional demands, extreme fatigue, weather exposure, hunger, or sleep deprivation, extended exposure to danger, loss, emotional/physical strain.[6]

The survivors were displaying the classic symptoms of confusion, disorientation, indecisiveness and poor judgement. However, the associated 'psychic numbing' or 'emotional anesthesia', along with the characteristic 'hyper vigilance' made it possible for them to carry on. For their lives now had only one purpose: to stay alive.

With great care and foreboding, the final match was deemed dry. They stood fearfully as Teer struck it and placed the tiny flame among the tinder, which this time they had carefully prepared. Sanguilly left the group at this point, as he could not bear to watch. It caught and the flame that would not be allowed to go out for almost two years flickered into life. Now they were able to prepare their first hot meal. They mixed pieces of two albatross killed on Disappointment Island with the contents of one of the precious tins of bouilli. 'This,' Teer wrote in the diary he kept scratched on sealskin, 'was our first meal after three days and two nights of suffering, and never did sumptuous repast taste better to a king than did this frugal meal to us. On the 17th gathered some limpets and made our breakfast. Having now but seven tins of bouilli, we kept them for cases of sickness.' Strengthened by food, they gathered branches to provide some slight protection from the wet ground and 'passed another miserable night, rain and sleet falling all the night'.[7]

The next day they rowed on southward along the shore, passing the basalt columns of Dea's Head. Then, blessedly, they saw a dilapidated hut. This was likely at Erebus Cove, site of the Hardwicke Settlement, near the entrance to Laurie Harbour.

> The site of the old settlement is situated on a low peninsula at the entrance to Laurie Cove. It is the most level spot on the whole island, and even this can hardly be called level as it consists of irregular mounds of peat, from which the dense scrub with which it was originally covered has been cleared away. The last vestiges of the old settlement have nearly disappeared...[8]

Leaving nine people to fix up this hut, the other boat kept on going and found more 'huts' along the shore towards Davis Island and Beacon

Point. Delighted, they headed back to give the others the good news. According to James Teer:

> Next morning, the 18th made a breakfast on limpets, when one of the boats started to explore, and the other boat started for the hut. This day Fortune again favored us. We killed four seals on the sandy beach at Enderby's Island; saw the goats, which the *Victoria* had landed there, but we did not succeed in catching any of them.[9]

In October 1865 the Commissioner of Trade and Customs in Melbourne had sent Captain W.H. Norman and the *Victoria* to the Aucklands 'for the purpose of searching for and relieving any person or persons who may be there and in distress'. The Victorian Acclimatisation Society, an organisation dedicated to introducing species of birds and animals to the new colonies, had arranged for animals to be taken to be let loose 'for any persons who may hereafter be wrecked or in distress upon these islands'. Norman was to take 'special stores . . . beyond the supply of ship's stores for three months (and exclusive of other fresh provisions) which you have laid in for 50 men, of which you will be good enough to take every care, and account for the same on your return to this port'.[10] These comprised:

25 pairs blankets	6 tomahawks
15 palliasses	1 case brandy
15 rugs	1 case port wine
20 men's complete suits	1 case sherry
10 women's complete suits	1 cask ale
boots and shoes of	1 cask porter
different sizes	1 cwt biscuits (tinned)
1 piece of flannel, about 50 yards	1 cwt soup & bouilli
1 piece of calico, about 25 yards	1 cwt preserved meat
3 tents	28 lbs arrowroot.

At some time during the intervening seven months this lifesaving stash had been stolen.

According to Teer's narrative, the survivors continued their difficult journey.

> Saturday, 19 – Pulled round Enderby's Island in search of Musgrave's hut, but we knew not at this time where it was situated. We intended

leaving no spot on the island without a thorough search, as we expected to find there a depot for clothing and provisions. I may here mention some of us were without shoes or stockings, while some had neither of these nor coats or hats to keep them warm in a cold and wet climate. We had four or five knives amongst us. Our only cooking utensils consisted of four or five empty bouilli tins. We were able to roast the seal on the fire, and boil some water so as to drink the broth, but the worst thing was the water tasted of salt.[11]

Shortly before the *General Grant* left Melbourne, the newspapers had been full of the miraculous survival of the five men of the *Grafton*, which had been overdue for two years. There are several versions as to what Thomas Musgrave, François-Edouard Raynal and their crew of three were doing on the Auckland Islands. For many years the story was that they had been on an unsuccessful prospecting trip for argentiferous tin to Campbell Island (this was supposedly reported by the crew of one of the Enderby vessels from the Hardwicke Settlement) and had put into Carnley Harbour at the extreme south end of the main Auckland Island to recoup some of the financial outlay by sealing.

In December 1934 and January 1935 there was a flurry of letters to the editor of the Melbourne *Age*, one of which was from Musgrave's son, who said that the *Grafton* crew had been prospecting on the Aucklands as well. Yet another writer said that they had gone to the islands to search for copper and anything else was just a cover story. Be that as it may, they penetrated deep into Carnley Harbour, past a point they christened the Musgrave Peninsula, and on into North Arm. Late in the afternoon of 1 January 1864, they dropped anchor in seven fathoms of water and, despite the shelter of the hills, Musgrave was worried. As darkness fell the wind changed to the north-west, funnelling over the hills and down the bay with great force. A second anchor was put out but to their horror one broke and the ship drifted ashore. They were fortunate, as they had the time to carry to safety:

Several bags of salt; Musgrave's chest, containing his charts, instruments of navigation, and the greater portion of his effects; mine, in which were my gun and sextant; a chest we had filled with useful domestic articles, such as plates, knives and forks; and a large iron pot, originally intended to melt the fat of the seals we felt so sure of killing.

Naturally we had carried with us, in preference to these, what remained of our supply of provisions: a small cask, containing nearly one hundred pounds of biscuit, and another which still held about fifty pounds of flour, nearly two pounds of tea, and three of coffee, enclosed in a couple of tin boxes; a little sugar, say one dozen pounds; a small quantity of salt meat, half a dozen (at the most) pieces of beef and two of pork; half a bottle of mustard; nearly a pound of pepper; a little salt; six pounds of American tobacco; and a small iron teakettle, which Harry, our cook, made use of for boiling fresh water.[12]

All these details had been given in the newspapers, so the *General Grant* survivors hoped that some of these items had been left behind and had not been pilfered by sealers. The articles had described the *Grafton* hut as a solid structure, 24 by 16 feet with a fireplace, chimney and stone sidewalls. If only they could find it.

On Monday 21 May, Teer and five crew – Morrison, Drew, McNevin, McClelland and Ferguson (despite his broken ribs) – set out to find the *Grafton* hut, leaving Jewell, Sanguilly, Caughey, Scott and Hayman with the passengers under Brown's supervision. Feelings had been running high between Teer and Brown after the match incident; this period apart would help to diffuse the tension. It was not a good trip: they were fog-bound for two days, and then became sick with dysentery. By the fourth day they had struggled to within five miles of Carnley Harbour, where snow, rain and wind forced them to take shelter once again. Teer later recounted what happened:

24th – Here we got a seal, but being all sick, we ate sparingly as we fancied the seal was unhealthy. We passed a miserable night, wet and cold. We found the remains of an old maimai [a rough hut] where we fancied some unfortunates like ourselves had camped.

25th – Took some raw seal and again started. On coming to the entrance of Musgrave's Bay, we were unable to go further. We did not know at this time this was the bay we were in search of, being so much reduced by toil and dysentery we gave up the search. We were so weak we could scarcely lift our oars out of the water. It was then we found relief from the piece of pork which had been for so long hoarded up. Some were unable, owing to sickness to eat of their small allowance; while those who ate it found relief and gained

strength, enabling us to pull to one of the bays, where we camped for
the night of the 26th.[13]

They then set off again, 'but were not able to reach home'. They camped
in a small bay about five miles to the north. 'Here we killed a seal. We
remained here till the 28th, when we arrived home. We found here were
all sick like ourselves; and, in fact, they were reduced to mere skeletons,
and we did not know each other after an absence of six days.' As Teer
concluded, 'All things have an end. It was wonderful to see how fast we
improved when we got a little used to our new mode of life. Still thought
Musgrave's hut could be found.' 'A new mode of life' – how much is
conveyed in that simple phrase. The hunt for food was the focus of their
day: 15 people had to be fed.

Hooker's sea lions were their staple diet and also provided them with
skins. Sea lion numbers had been much reduced by sealers, but Jewell
was to estimate that they killed 1000 of the mammals during their stay
on the island. The big bulls are massive creatures, weighing up to 340
pounds. The older 'beachmasters', with great manes, raise themselves on
their front flippers to the height of a man as they protect their harems
of doe-eyed blonde females. Although they are ocean creatures, their
hind limbs or flippers turn forward, making it possible for them to move
surprisingly quickly on land. The island is laced with sea lion trails. The
bulls, particularly during the mating season, can be quite threatening
but are rarely known to carry through an attack, depending instead on a
series of quick dashes and a loud roar. Their weak spot is the skull at the
base of the nose, and a hard blow with a stick will kill a sea lion quickly.

Once killed, a sea lion had to be carved up and brought back to
camp. The blowflies, their metallic blue-green abdomens bulging with
eggs, followed the survivors everywhere so in no time the meat would
be putrid and covered with maggots. These flies are notorious on the
islands, blowing almost everything in sight, from clothing to a knife
blade. It was not until the castaways found an old boiler and were able to
concentrate salt that they were able to make any effort at preserving the
meat. They attributed their dysentery to bad meat, but Robert Holding
of the *Invercauld* and others wrecked on the Aucklands concluded that
illness was caused by eating the livers of the sea lions and that once these
were eliminated from their diet their health improved.

The sea, of course, held a wealth of food. The shores are lined with
beds of the huge blue mussel, and limpets line the rocks, but it did not
take 15 people long to clean out the local stocks. Jewell described how

they made fishing lines out of flax and fishhooks from nails found on the settlement site. The islands are a true sanctuary for birds – albatross, shags, prions and Cape pigeons, all nesting on the cliffs or on the tops.

Finally, there was the overwhelming need for rest and a sense of security. In May, night falls early in those latitudes and the long, long hours would be spent huddled around the tiny fire before they took to their damp beds. The woods were full of night noises – pigs screaming and rooting, sea lions moving through the bushes – and sleep was also interrupted by the need to watch the fire, and by sheer discomfort. Night after night, the same dreary pattern. They would awaken from restless sleep to another day of harsh reality.

The Hardwicke settlers had not been the only ones to make their home on the islands. When Enderby and his settlers sailed into Port Ross they had been greeted by about 40 Maori and their 30 Moriori slaves, who had arrived several years before from the Chatham Islands after internal discord there. Their pa (settlements) were located around Laurie Harbour; there was also a small one on Enderby Island. They, too, were defeated by the weather and left not long after the settlers. Except for the flax they had planted, all signs of their sojourn had vanished.

Teer, always practical, kept trying new ideas.

> During this time, some of those barefooted tried to make shoes out of the seal's skin, but did not succeed very well. One day I thought of the moccasin and made a pair for P. McNevin. Soon after this all hands were able to make them for themselves. These were good substitutes during our stay on the island.
>
> I made some needles from the bone of the albatross; also some salt. The salt was made in a piece of an old broken pot, which I found at the hut. It held half a pint of water at a time; therefore, the quantity made was small and useless.[14]

After the experience of rowing around to Port Ross and down towards Carnley Harbour, the castaways tried to make a sail of flax; they later had more success with stitching sealskins together. Once a sail had been made, one of the boats set off on 26 June to search for Musgrave's hut. Teer was unwell, so did not go. 'After much suffering from the inclemency of weather and camping out in the rain, snow and wet, the long looked for hut was found on the 11th of July.' But rather than 'a well stocked depot [they] found nothing of value except an old boiler, afterwards used to boil salt in and some old canvass which lined the inside of the hut, all else having been carried away'. The boat returned on 13 July.

While that boat was away, Teer and others had searched 'around home' with the second boat. 'We found the papers and trees marked by the *Victoria* and *Southland* at the old settlement, where we learned that there was nothing of any value to us left by them and that we might give up all hopes of either steamers returning to these two islands. Saw some pig tracks at the head of the bay, but no pigs. When the boat returned, they were all well, and when we were told what was left in the hut, we offered up many a hearty prayer.' The next day, 14 July, some of those who had been away

> wished to see the papers left by the steamers; went to the settlement and while there they were fortunate enough to find an oven belonging to a stove; this made a good pot for cooking in. During the boat's absence we visited a small island [later identified as Rose Island], lying between Enderby's and the main island where an old hut was found all ready fitted up with three bunks, some wearing apparel, a few old bouilli tins, an old adze, and a spade. The hut appeared as though recently vacated, as the hind part of a seal was still hanging to a tree. Rabbits were very numerous but we had no means of catching any; we gave it the name Rabbit Island.[15]

Robert Holding, a survivor of the *Invercauld* wreck, had helped to build this hut and had left it only 14 months before when he and his fellow castaways were rescued by the *Julian* after 375 days on the island. But the seal carcass indicated much more recent occupation. It would not have lasted even a month with the scavenger birds and flies. Is it possible that they missed seeing someone? Another mystery of the islands. The number of other items found around the settlement also hinted that others had possibly stayed there during the intervening months, for the *Invercauld* survivors had scoured every inch of the area.

The *General Grant* survivors had now been on the island for three months, Musgrave's hut had been found; it was time for some major decisions. The crew returning from Carnley Harbour wanted everyone to go down to live there as the hut was much bigger than the Port Ross shelter and the seals were more plentiful. The drawback of this plan was that they would all be moving to an area where they would have no view of the open sea. This was the very situation that had driven three of the *Grafton*'s crew, Musgrave, Raynal and a crewman, Alick MacLaren, to attempt to sail for New Zealand in an 11-foot boat. Before the Carnley group headed back to the harbour on 19 July, they decided that if rescue had not come in six months, some of them would attempt to emulate Musgrave's feat and go for help.

The constant search for food continued. They had to battle the wind and waves of the open harbour to get to Enderby Island where, one day, they captured a goat and two kids and somehow managed to bring them back in the open boat. These animals shared the hut with them, adding, perhaps, a little warmth.

Walking on the islands was difficult – everywhere. The area that had been cleared 13 years before was now covered with young growth of rata, olearia, myrsine and dracophyllum. The pebble paths through the settlement no longer provided a clear way for they had partially sunk into the peaty soil. Further back from the shore, where the mature rata intertwined in fantastic shapes, and gullies and depressions were blocked with ferns and the broad-leaved olearia, movement was almost impossible. Branches tore at their clothing; rocks cut their boots and sealskin moccasins. Despite the albatross bone needles and thread made from flax, they had to do something to replace the clothing that was literally falling off their backs. Teer described their efforts:

> We tried every means to manufacture seal's skin into clothes, as those we had left were all threadbare, and the skins we had to keep us warm at night were like boards. We scrubbed them with sand, and scraped them with glass but to no purpose. At last I hit upon a successful plan, I was trying to get a patch for my trousers, and thought of paring the skins with a knife, but I cut out a hole in every square inch; I saw the plan would answer by paring the dried skins close to the roots of the hair; the skin was then very soft, and by perseverance and practice I found that we would be able to make clothes much better than we imagined.[16]

The two groups kept in regular contact, despite the 40-mile trip in each direction. On 19 September, Teer recorded, 'after seven weeks of very severe weather, the boat returned from Musgrave's bringing some seal, thinking we might be short, owing to their scarcity, but they found us all right'. This time Teer went back with them for a short period. He and the others were taken ill with a strange malady known to whalers as cobbler.

Nearly all of us were taken sick with a swelling of the limbs, which commenced at the stomach and worked its way to the legs and feet, rendering them almost helpless. At first thought it was the scurvy, as the swollen parts when any pressure came upon them retained the indentation made for quite a long time.[17]

Several weeks later Teer returned and life continued. 'The weather being fine we were able to go about in search of anything useful. On Enderby's we killed some fur seal, the skins of which we pared and made blankets. We found a couple of files, a gun flint, and one or two knives at the old huts.' The *Invercauld* hut had obviously been used by others since Holding, Dalgarno and Andrew Smith were rescued. Whaling and sealing gangs landed on the islands from time to time, and perhaps there had been other, unrecorded shipwrecks. The finding of the flint lifted a great weight from their minds: should the fire be extinguished, they could now rekindle it.

Then on 6 October, after almost five months of searching an empty horizon, they saw a sail to the north-west. Joseph Jewell described what happened:

Two out of the seven men at Port Ross were very ill at the time, and you can imagine our joy at seeing the ship. It was a very fine day, which is an exception in that part of the world, and we all took a trip to a small island [Rose Island]. I left my wife and one of the sick men to light signal fires, while four of us started in chase of the vessel, and we got within two miles of her; then the wind freshened and she passed on without taking any notice either of us in the boat or the fires on shore, and I am sure they must have seen the smoke. It was dark when we got back to the island, weary and disappointed after our hard day's pull. I found my wife careworn and depressed, and the few clothes she had on were torn to pieces while she was gathering bushes and grass to keep the signal fires alight. The ship was a large one, and, I believe, home-ward bound.[18]

Those were harsh times and captains had been known to maroon trouble-makers. Although morality would point to aiding castaways, a prudent captain might think twice about risking his passengers and ship.

The search for food went on, as Teer recounted: 'This caused visits to be paid to Rabbit Island very often. There we got a number of rabbits by knocking them over with sticks. As spring set in we got some sea-fowl eggs, which were a great change, and caught quite a number of fish. About November 1st we caught another goat . . . .'

On 8 December, the other boat returned from Carnley for good.

> We were at this time able to make coats, vests and trousers out of the seal's skin. Those who had been at Musgrave's had nothing made of seal's skin, but after making some sails for the boat they patched up their clothes with the remaining pieces of canvas.
>
> One day while at the old huts, which had been burned, when gathering nails, found an axe; and the same day those at home got one in the stump of an old tree in front of the hut we lived in. We commenced to fit up the boat for a passage to New Zealand, as before the summer was over she was expected to start.[19]

William Scott, Andrew Morrison, Peter McNevin and Bart Brown offered to attempt to reach New Zealand. Brown, still inconsolable over the loss of his wife, 'volunteered to go in the boat with the serene cheerfulness of a man whose only wish was to die'.[20] The survivors did what they could to prepare the little 22-two foot pinnace for the open ocean, covering it with sealskins and equipping it with a sail made from canvas stripped from the walls of Musgrave's hut. It was provisioned for a three-week voyage, even though the trip should take no longer than three or four days. Dried seal gullets were filled with water; 20 pounds of seal flesh, a few dozen cooked sea fowl eggs, the seven tins of soup and bouilli and the meat from a goat and two kids were carefully stowed; a small charcoal stove was also included.

On 22 January 1867 the four men set out with the prayers and hopes of the 11 left on shore. It seems inconceivable that they would even contemplate such a voyage without compass or chart, and without even knowing the course they were to steer. As Teer later commented sadly, 'they thought that steering east north east would bring them to New Zealand, but since we have learned that the course was north, or a little to the west of north'. He continued:

> When the boat left the wind was S.W. but it shifted the first night to the N.W. with rain. It blew very hard most of the night. On the 23rd it shifted to the S.W. and remained so till the 29th with fine weather, giving them ample time to reach New Zealand if they survived that first night. There is a possibility that they might have made Campbell Islands, as they are about 200 miles in an easterly direction, if so they

are most likely there still. [Since 160 nautical miles equals 185 statute miles, they must have at least seen a chart of the area.] After the boat was away about five weeks we began to give her up, and thought of keeping a look-out on Enderby's for passing ships, and where seal might be procured without the constant use of the boat, which we were obliged to take great care of.

Teer now became the undisputed leader of the group and was later credited, in a large part, for their survival.

8th March – Went to Enderby's and built two huts, also built a small hut for a lookout station, where a look-out was kept from daylight till

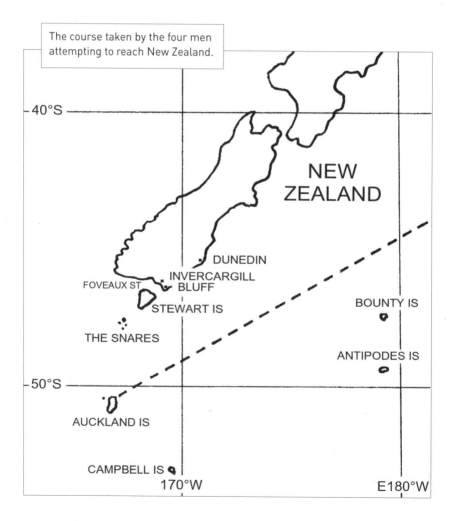

The course taken by the four men attempting to reach New Zealand.

dark all the time we were on the island, the men taking it in turn.

On the 23rd of April we gathered a pile of wood for lighting as a signal, in case a ship was seen. When the huts were being built we went to North Harbor in search of boards along the beach, and saw quite a number of pigs. We caught a small one, and within five or six feet of several large ones but could catch none. Any sort of weapon would have been of great use. Seal being very plentiful on Enderby's we had but little trouble in procuring enough to eat.

Before the winter set in we went to Musgrave's and brought some casks, and the old boiler for making salt in. Salted some seal down, and it was well we did so, as the winter was very severe. Had we been living at the old hut we should probably have been obliged quite often to have gone with out anything to eat, as there were three or four weeks together when the boat could not have been used.[21]

As they were combing the shore on Enderby Island, they found a barrel stave which had written on it in charcoal: '*Minerva* – 4 men, 1 officer – Leith, May 10 1864 and March 25 1865'. The name that followed was illegible. This artifact was to cause no end of confusion and it was not until Robert Holding's manuscript came to light in 1997 that a connection with the *Invercauld* was made. The supposition now is that the stave did possibly come from a vessel called the *Minerva* but the date was that of the wreck of the *Invercauld*. The reference to '4 men, 1 officer' continues to be a mystery: both the mate and the skipper from the *Invercauld* survived, along with one seaman.

The stamina of the castaways throughout the long months had been outstanding. Despite cold, threat of starvation and the roughest shelter imaginable, they had all survived. Then, sadly, on 3 September 1867, the 62-year-old Glaswegian, David McLelland, unexpectedly 'departed this life'. He was laid in a grave facing Port Ross. According to Sir Robert Falla, it is possible that McLelland was buried in the cemetery in Port Ross (or initially on Enderby Island, then disinterred some time later and buried in the Port Ross Cemetery).[22] It is believed that later a piece of slate marked 'unknown' was hung on a bush above this grave by the crew of a visiting vessel.

Their optimism was shaken by the loss of McClelland, but the remaining 10 survivors did not give up hope. Teer, ever the innovator, came up with an idea for capturing pigs. Using an old cannon ball as an anvil, he fashioned a foot-long half-inch bolt into a hook which he tied onto a rope made of flax. This was then attached to a 10-foot pole.

A few days later, we saw pigs on the beach, tried the hook and found it a success. I hooked a fine sow, the rod pulling from the fastening of the hook, leaving her fast to the rope; also caught a small one. Three or four weeks later, on going along the shore we got another pig. We had not our hooks ready but as he took to the water we caught him by means of the boat. Next day were prepared with our hooks – saw seven and caught three, proving the success of our weapon for pig hunting. Two days after this went to North Harbour, or as we have name it; Pig Bay. Killed two large pigs and brought home nine small ones alive. Had we been accustomed to the hooks we would have got many more. Following week killed seven and brought five small ones alive home. Were not out again for two weeks; this time was taken up in fixing our pig-yards and in planting our potatoes.[23]

After 15 months of living on nothing but seal, pork was a great delicacy. A number of pigs, among them a boar called Roger and a sow called Nellie, became quite tame and were kept as pets.

The descendants of the pigs left by Bristow in 1807, Sir James Clark Ross, the famous Antarctic explorer, in 1840 and the Chatham Island Maori in 1842 have interbred and bear very little resemblance to slow-moving, pink domestic pigs. They are big and bold with an almost spiny coat that ranges from white through tan and brown to black. They are not unlike the 'Captain Cookers' of New Zealand. When the Rare Breeds Society brought some back to New Zealand in 1999, they were described as 'very athletic'.

Although unpopular at the time, James Teer was later credited by his fellow castaways as their saviour. He forced them to eat grass and other greenery as an anti-scorbutic. He constructed a ramp over which he forced them to run and jump before going to bed so as to stimulate their circulation. Standing alongside with a whip made of platted sealskin to provide encouragement, he made them repeat the exercise over and over. A big man, he enforced his orders physically if he deemed it necessary.

As the days since the departure of Brown and the others turned into weeks, all hope that their comrades had reached New Zealand vanished.

About this time we sent off a small boat in the hope that some vessel might pick it up, and thus learn of our existence. We subsequently sent off another small boat and at various times we sent off inflated bladders of the pigs and goats we killed with a slip of wood attached to them. The boats were formed of a rough piece of wood, about three feet long, to which by way of keel, I attached a heavy piece of iron so as to trim the little craft by the stern, to keep her before the wind, a short stout mast with a tin sail completed the little vessel. On the deck of the boat was carved the ship's name, date, and place of wreck, number of survivors, and the date on which the boat itself was launched. The same particulars were also punched with a nail into the tin sail and carved on the labels attached to the bladders. We also put the words 'want relief' on the bows of the boats and on the sails and labels. [One of these boats is now in the collection of the Southland Museum, Invercargill.][24]

By November, the seals were becoming scarce and they redoubled their efforts to capture pigs for breeding and for salting down for the long winter, which they feared would find them still on the islands. Then a sail was sighted on 19 November, six weeks after David McClelland died. Unfortunately, the boat was away and all those on shore could do was light the signal fires and watch helplessly as the ship faded eastward into the fog. Their disappointment was palpable as they once more prepared the brush for burning.

The weather turned squally, with winds sweeping the waters of the harbour into angry swells. Late in the afternoon of 21 November their hopes soared as they saw another ship coming from the south, apparently making for Enderby Island. While some ran with brands from the home fire to the piles by the shore and on the heights, the others launched the boat and rowed furiously towards the approaching ship. Contact at last! Those on shore watched with joy as the men were taken aboard. It was after dark before the *Amherst* dropped anchor in Sarah's Bosom. Those still on Enderby could only look across the bay to the welcoming lights before crawling into their hut for one last night. In the morning, the ship's pinnace landed on the beach. Their long wait was over.

With true understatement Joseph Jewell told his parents that 'the brig, "Amhurst" [*sic*], Captain Gillroy [*sic*] of Invercarjale [*sic*], came into Port Ross and rescued us from our miserable condition, and words cannot express the joy we felt when we arrived on the vessel's deck'.[25] One of the seamen on the *Amherst* noted the sad condition of the castaways: 'Many of the party were unable to run, from continued wet feet, their legs having become swollen to twice their ordinary size, the sinews completely callused, and were at this time fit subjects for hospital treatment.'[26]

The next day some made one final trip back to Enderby to organise the items they had collected and to let the pigs go. With the assistance of the *Amherst* crewmen, the boat was pulled clear of the water and placed on blocks. The *Amherst*'s skipper, Irishman Paddy Gilroy, was well known in southern New Zealand maritime circles and is mentioned in Frank Bullen's great book on whaling, *The Cruise of the Cachalot*. He filled a tin case with a knife, a box of matches, fishhooks, twine for fishing lines, a gun, a box of caps, shot, lead, bullet mould, paper, pencil, flint and steel and a boat compass. Beside it he placed a bottle containing the following message: 'These articles are left at the suggestion of the survivors of the *General Grant*, who found their need of them in their destitute condition'. Gilroy also put in a sealed cask a selection of books: a Bible, a New Testament, *Looking to the Cross, 12 Lectures of St. Paul, On Prayer, British Messenger, Sunday at Home,* Spurgeon's *Sermons* and Watts's *Hymns and Psalms*. It was an interesting and perhaps unusual collection to be culled from the library of a sealing vessel.

Two slate memorials were placed beside the Victoria tree. One read:

> Sacred to the memory of 68 persons, who lost their lives by the wreck of the General Grant, on the morning of the 14th of May, 1866, on the Auckland Islands.

The other bore these words:

> Sacred to the memory of Bart Brown, Wm N Scott, A.B., Andrew Morrison, A.B., Peter McNevin, A.B., who started in a boat on the 22nd January, 1867, for New Zealand, without chart, compass or nautical instrument – Blessed are they that die in the Lord.

On the back of the latter was inscribed: '10 survivors, rescued by the brig Amherst, of Invercargill, New Zealand, Patrick Gilroy, master. 21st November, 1867'.

Rescue had been imminent from another quarter, as Teer noted in his final diary entry:

> December 5 – We saw the *Fanny* (cutter) in Carnley's Harbor. The captain having seen the papers left by the *Victoria* at Musgrave's, on the back of which we had written our names, where we were, and the name of ship in which we were wrecked, had put his casks ashore,

The *General Butler*, built to the same general design as the *General Grant*.
(Maine Maritime Museum)

An artist's impression of the wreck of the *General Grant*, based on a sketch
by one of the survivors. (*New Zealand Herald*, April 1868. Hocken Library)

James Teer, who survived the wreck and became a leader of the castaways.

(*Otago Daily Times and Witness*, November 1899. Alexander Turnbull Library)

Joseph and Mary Ann Jewell, the only married couple to survive the wreck.

(*Wide World Magazine*, January 1899)

David Ashworth survived the wreck but died while searching for the gold on the *Daphne* expedition in 1870.

(*Otago Witness*. Hocken Library)

Patrick Caughey, survivor of the wreck and a boyhood friend of James Teer.

(*Otago Daily Times and Witness*, November 1899. Alexander Turnbull Library)

The hut built by the survivors. Note the animal pens to the right of the hut, where Roger and Nellie, the tame pigs, were housed.
(Archives New Zealand)

An artist's impression of the meeting between James Teer and Captain Paddy Gilroy on the deck of the *Amherst*, which finally rescued the survivors.
(*Wide World Magazine*, January 1899)

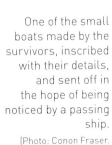

One of the small boats made by the survivors, inscribed with their details, and sent off in the hope of being noticed by a passing ship.
(Photo: Conon Fraser. Southland Museum)

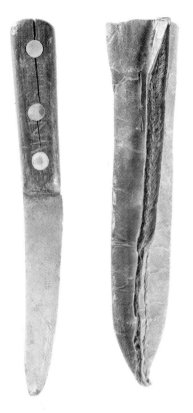

Sheath knife and sealskin sheath owned by survivor W. N. Scott – his name and the date 'May 1866' are carved on the handle. Scott was one of the four survivors lost in a vain attempt to reach New Zealand in a ship's boat.

(Te Papa: Museum of New Zealand)

One of the two slate memorial plaques placed by the survivors beside the *Victoria* tree on Auckland Island. This one commemorates the 68 people lost in the original shipwreck.

(Photo: Conon Fraser. Southland Museum)

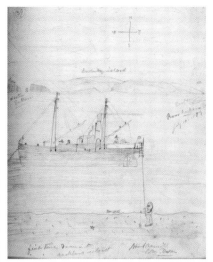

Diver G.H. Sherwill's drawing of diving on the wreck site, from his 'Log of the SS *Gazelle*', 1877.
(Invercargill Public Library)

The crew of the *Enterprise*, 1916. The two standing figures are Percy Catling and Jack Olsen (right).
(*Otago Witness*, Hocken Library)

The 'Cavern of Death' from the deck of the *Enterprise*.
(*Otago Witness*, Hocken Library)

Philatelic covers issued for various *General Grant* expeditions: Catling's expedition, 1915 (Madelene Allen Collection); Kelly Tarlton's cancelled expedition, 1983 (Madelene Allen Collection); the *Little Mermaid* expedition, 1986. (Malcolm Blair Collection)

Bill Havens aboard the *Goldseeker* before departure from England, 1955.
(Photo: Havens family)

R.V. *Acheron* off the western coast of Auckland Island in 1975 with a moderate sea running. This site is that of the *Anjou* wreck (1905).
(Archives New Zealand)

At first John Grattan and Kelly Tarlton both believed this anchor was from
the *General Grant*, but Tarlton later changed his mind. It eventually proved to
be the anchor of the *Anjou* wrecked in 1905.

(Photo: John Dearling)

John Dearling, veteran diver of three *General Grant* expeditions, displays
two silver half-crowns from the Half Crown Wreck site and a small
bronze bulkhead bracket from the *Anjou* wreck (1905).

(Photo: John Dearling)

Back in Bluff Harbour, Kelly Tarlton displays the anchor recovered from the 'Cavern of Death' in 1970. It turned out to be the anchor from the *Enterprise* lost by Catling's expedition 54 years earlier.

(Photo: John Dearling)

Commander John Grattan, who was involved in three expeditions to find the gold of the *General Grant*.

(Archives New Zealand)

The crew of the 1975 O'Farrell expedition on R.V. *Acheron*.
Back row: Kelly Tarlton, Joe McCormack, John Grattan, Terry McCormack.
Front row: Alex Black (skipper), John Dearling.

(Photo: John Dearling)

and was on the way to look for us when we saw him. For this we feel greatly thankful to Captain Ackers and the crew of the *Fanny*.

It would be 13 January before the survivors set foot in New Zealand. Certainly, they were beholden to Captain Gilroy for their rescue, but they must surely have resented being carried as so much baggage while the *Amherst* continued her sealing voyage. After all, the Aucklands were, at a maximum, two and a half days' sailing time from Bluff. One wonders at Gilroy's motivation for not losing a week by taking them back, rather than finding places for them to sleep and having to feed 10 more mouths. Eunson suggests that they would have been grateful for the opportunity to 'adjust to new people and new conditions, to become used again to a normal diet and to enjoy the luxury of tobacco smoke trickling through their lips and the sweet taste of sugar on their palates',[27] but for another six weeks their loved ones mourned. It seems hard to believe that, after having been castaways for 18 months, they were really so magnanimous as to insist that Gilroy continue his sealing.

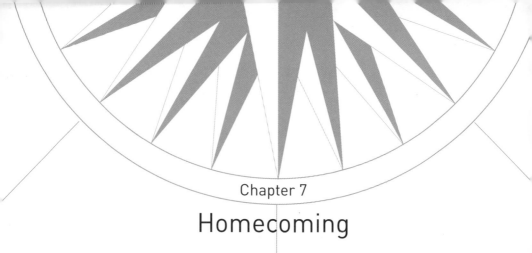

Chapter 7

Homecoming

The Invercargill telegraph operator, stirred from his Monday morning reverie, wrote down in pencil the message from Bluff as it unfolded from the chattering Morse code keys, telling of yet another Auckland Island disaster, but this time there was the miraculous survival of 10 persons, 'including a woman'. This was the first that was heard of a story that would echo around the world and down through the years for well over a century. A messenger hurried to the mayor's home with the news and within the hour a special train filled with dignitaries, including the wife of the Superintendent of Southland Province, John Parkin Taylor, who was to take charge of Mrs Jewell, steamed down the track to Bluff, 18 miles to the south-east. The word spread quickly through the town and surrounding countryside, and by five o'clock the crowd, which had begun to gather at noon, filled the platform. Bewildered and exhausted, the survivors descended to cheers and outstretched hands.

Finally, breaking away from the welcoming crowd, they were taken to the local hotel where, at last, they were able to have a hot bath before adjusting to the unaccustomed comfort of real beds. Offers of help poured in from all over Southland and further afield; churches and community organisations arranged fundraisers. When the word spread of the four men who had set off in the boat, a public meeting, hosted by the mayor and local dignitaries, was held to discuss the possibility of sending an expedition to the Aucklands and other subantarctic islands to search for the missing men and any others who might be stranded. The provincial government pledged £200 towards the project and plans were set in motion to collect donations throughout New Zealand and Australia.

Up to this point there had been no regular visits to the Aucklands and a proposal was put forward that the government should be asked to consider such a patrol, considering that this was the second time within two and a half years that a group of castaways had arrived in Invercargill after an extended time on these remote islands. The New Zealand Parliament mooted the idea of erecting a lighthouse to warn wayward ships. In a letter to the editor of the *Southland Times*, J.P. Meadows made several other suggestions:

> Sir – being an eyewitness to the pitiful condition of the survivors of the ill-fated ship *General Grant* alone induces me to pen the following – that action may be taken by the authorities without delay to do something more than has hitherto been done to alleviate the sufferings of those who may in future be castaway on those Islands.
>
> I would respectfully suggest that a beacon (of stone, being easily procurable and lasting) be erected on the most suitable position at Port Ross, and that a depot of the following provisions be deposited in hermetically sealed packages, viz. Flour, oatmeal, biscuit, tea, sugar, blankets, slops, axes, tomahawks, matches, medicines, and a few useful books, writing materials, and the last, but not least, to distribute through the islands (and they might be placed with advantage on the Campbells, Antipodes, and Bounty Islands) a few dozen of native emus (commonly known as wood emus); being natives of a similar climate, hardy, prolific, nutritious, and easily caught, they would be a more ready means of substance to shipwrecked persons than hunting for seal and pigs. The island also abounds with food suitable for them.[1]

Whether his letter spurred government action or not, it was prophetic, for shortly afterwards castaway depots were established on the islands. (Incidentally, the wood emus suggested by Meadows were in fact New Zealand weka.)

On the morning of Monday 15 January 1868, with great fanfare, the official inquiry into the sinking opened in the Bluff courthouse. Lee Street was thronged with people waiting to catch sight of the now famous group of 10 and to see the magistrate, I.N. Watt, and the nautical adviser, Captain Waldron, of the *Ethel*.

> The rescued crew mustered outside the Court-house, awaiting their turn to give evidence, formed a picturesque group, with their Robinson Crusoe-looking dress, and weather-beaten, but not bronzed faces – the climate of the Aucklands has too little sunshine for that.

The female passenger, too, was there, once more dressed in civilized costume, looking rosy, and happy as possible.[2]

Local citizen A.J. Smyth, 'with much kindness', insisted that William Sanguilly, 'a most intelligent and vivacious young American sailor', accept his offer 'of the best rig-out to be had in Campbelltown' (as Bluff was also known). Now suitably attired, Billy Sanguilly took his place in the box as the first witness.

> The court listened entranced as this young man, barely twenty years of age, spoke clearly of what he had experienced. He described the ship, its cargo and the fact that the captain had not been able to take sightings for several days before the wreck and the weather as they sighted the island. 'The wind had fallen to a dead calm, the ship drifted into a cove on the coast, at the end of which was a cave, about 400 yards, situated on the west coast of the Main island.' He stated that they had 'never been to the wreck since we left her, our boats and weather prevented us'.[3]

Next came William Ferguson, the able seaman who had been at the wheel of the *General Grant* when she grounded. 'I have been at sea for twelve years and from my experience, I think all that could possibly be done was done to wear the ship off the land. I don't know whether the ship was insured. The captain and officers were sober; no disturbance that I know of arose on board from the time we left Melbourne.'

Mary Ann Jewell made it very clear that she was a paying passenger but told how she had to sign articles as a stewardess so that she could accompany her husband, and in fact 'no person on board acted as stewardess'. She confirmed Sanguilly's testimony that there had been 'no disturbance' on board.

The last witness was James Teer, identified as 'a Mariner by trade', but travelling as a passenger, and so an excellent witness to speak for both the crew and passengers as to the ability of the officers and crew.

> Everything possible was done to keep the ship off; in fact, the captain went so far as to ask the advice of some of the passengers whom he thought capable of forming an opinion; told me he could not get an observation for forty-eight hours, or he would not have been so near the land ... The cave being only a little broader than the ship, she

chafed her bilges against the sides, and also the stump of her main mast bumping against the roof, which, I think must have penetrated through her bottom, are the causes of the ship sinking.

For the newspapermen present this story had it all – death, drama, pathos, tragedy, heroism and a mysterious cargo of gold – and they gave it everything they had.

> Of the horrors of that awful night, spent in that dismal vault, with the groaning, straining ship, and the angry, sullen splash of the surging water ever sounding in their ears, those only who have escaped can form a just conception. At last the never doubtful contest between wood and iron and rock is over – the struggles of the ship have but hastened her own destruction – the roof of the cave has forced her mast through her bottom, and the hungry waters rush in. Slowly she fills, and settles down, down; the people crowd her poop, but no hope. Still the waters rise, and none can save her. At last she gives a shiver, a plunge; there is one long, wild shriek, and all is over – the *General Grant* has disappeared forever, and her living freight left struggling with the seething waters. Of the eighty-three souls who but a short while before were full of life, and life's busy projects, and all the hopes and anticipations incident to a homeward voyage, only fifteen survived the wreck of the ship, and gained a landing on the island.[4]

Illustrators, too, aimed for maximum drama. The most famous depiction of the *General Grant* 'staggering under full sail into a mammoth cave' appeared in the *London Illustrated News* soon after the news of the wreck reached England. Southland Provincial Government representative Henry Armstrong was not impressed: 'My faith has been rather shaken in pictorial accuracy ever since, and my belief strengthened in the imagination of artists.'

The final verdict of the court of inquiry was 'Wreck an accident; no blame attributable to anyone on board'. The following remarks were added:

> Fifteen souls in all were saved from this ill-fated vessel, but one died on the Auckland Islands, and four, who left in a boat in search of aid, were never more heard of. The ten survivors were landed at Bluff Harbour, on Jan. 13, 1868, one year and eight months after the date of the wreck. They were kindly treated by their rescuer, Captain

Gilroy, of the brig 'Amherst' who deserves some public recognition of
his humane conduct.[5]

No attempts were made to second-guess Captain Loughlin or his officers
over what other actions could have been taken to save the ship or reduce
the loss of life. Eunson discusses two interesting options: first, had the
crew cut down the masts when the ship first struck, they would not have
holed the hull, and second, if Loughlin had known the local weather
pattern of the wind dropping at night and picking up in the morning he
would have evacuated the ship immediately rather than waiting for dawn.
However, wind dropping at night is common in both hemispheres, and
putting boats over the side in total darkness would have been extremely
dangerous.[6]

In the years that followed, there was considerable discussion as
to whether the charts used by the *General Grant* had the Aucklands
misplaced by 24 miles. (Some references say 25 miles, others up to 36.)
Bristow had the latitude and longitude almost exactly right. Henry
Armstrong wrote to the Victorian government to inform them that there
was an error on the 1851 British Imray chart. However, the fifth edition
of the *Directory for the Navigation of South Pacific Ocean*, published in
London in 1871, states very clearly 'that it was a vague assertion, for
which there is not the shadow of an excuse'.[7] The chart published by
the American hydrographical expert M.F. Maury in 1858 had shown
the Cape Horn route running to the north of the Auckland Islands (but
the Islands themselves were not marked at all), despite the fact that the
United States Naval Exploring Expedition in the *Porpoise* went to the
area from 1838 to 1842 with the specific task of making 'adequate' charts
and 'to supply useful information concerning the islands of Pacific and
seas of Antarctica'.[8] The *Porpoise* actually visited the Auckland Islands
in 1840.

It is not inconceivable that Captain Loughlin was using the Maury
chart although the castaways made straight for Laurie Harbour, not
stopping in North Harbour, the first deep bay, nor at North Point. Some
of them had also gone south to Carnley Harbour as soon as they were
physically able. Had they not seen some other chart it is unlikely that
they would have done either of these things so quickly.

After the inquiry, the survivors were offered free passage back to
Melbourne on the *Otago*. Arriving safely in Australia, they were dismayed
to find that the Victorian government was unable to do anything for
them as the *General Grant* was an American ship, and so they were all

considered 'foreigners'. A subscription was made and each received £5 11s 5d. As David Ashworth commented, 'It was not enough to pay for our board, much less clothing that we were in need of – only having the suit that we received in Southland.'[9]

Apart from James Teer, David Ashworth and Cornelius Drew, all of whom returned to the islands on three separate expeditions, and Mary Ann and Joseph Jewell, who took to the lecture circuit for a brief time, little is known about the other survivors. Aaron Hayman, terrified of ever boarding a ship again, settled and married in Australia, Sanguilly went back to Boston and Nicholas Allen is said to have gone to the United States.

There are three principal first-hand accounts of the wreck of the *General Grant* by the survivors: those by James Teer, Joseph Jewell and William Sanguilly.

No transcripts of the Jewells' talks survive. Newspaper articles, which appeared elsewhere, appear to have been taken almost verbatim from the *Southland Times*' coverage. William Sanguilly spoke to the press in the United States and a brief account was published in *Harpers Weekly Magazine* in 1869.

In an era known for popular non-fiction, when books of travel and adventure rolled off the presses, no full-length published account of the *General Grant* was published. Teer later gave lectures on the West Coast but why did more of the survivors not take advantage of their story? Many of them had lost everything in the wreck and could have used even the meagre income from a published book.

Thomas Musgrave and F.E. Raynal of the *Grafton* both published journals. Musgrave's appeared in 1865 in Australia and in London in 1866 under the title, *Castaway on the Auckland Isles* and Raynal's account, *Les Naufrages ou Vingt Mois sur un Récif des Iles Auckland*, was published in Paris in 1870. It was translated into English in 1882 and published as *Wrecked on a Reef*. Of the 19 men who made it ashore from the *Invercauld* in 1864, only three survived to be rescued a year later. Andrew Smith, the first mate, told their story in *The Castaways*, published in Scotland in 1866; Robert Holding, the seaman, typed his manuscript in 1926, which eventually evolved into *Wake of the* Invercauld in 1997. Captain Dalgarno, however, never published his promised account. Four years after the *Dundonald* was lost in 1907, *Castaways of Disappointment Island*, written by the Reverend H. Escott-Inman, based on information supplied by survivor Charles Eyre, was published. Raynal and Musgrave were both well educated; Andrew Smith and Robert Holding were both self-educated. Surely one of the *General Grant* survivors had the skills to write a book.

It would be unreasonable to think that 15 people from such diverse backgrounds – rough seamen, businessmen, miners, and one woman; four passengers and 11 crew – would have been able live together in complete harmony under such conditions for 18 months. To some extent the group was divided from the first day for Teer and Brown were both men of strong character with considerable experience and each had their following. Teer, having had considerable maritime experience, understood seamen and held some sway with them. Nicholas Allen's lot was not an enviable one, for everyone knew he had left his wife and children to their fate. He was the only married man to survive other than Joseph Jewell, who lived only because he had leapt into the sea to help his wife into the boat.

The decision that half of the group would go to live at Carnley is a strange one. Certainly this resulted in more room and less drain on the local food supply, but this group deliberately put themselves in a location where it was impossible to see the open sea. They were depending almost completely on the northern group sighting a ship, being rescued and then coming south for them. Perhaps, had all things been equal, they would have wanted to stay together for mutual support.

Almost a century and a half has passed since the events on the Aucklands, and still stories are trickling out as descendants speak of long-hidden family secrets that the survivors perhaps vowed never to tell, which may account for the fact that no full contemporary published account was ever written.

How many actually survived the wreck? We have only the statements of the survivors. As in many castaway sagas, where the possibility of starvation was constantly in the background, the question of turning to cannibalism arose. Sanguilly told of such a discussion which concluded that they would cast lots for the victim. As an American, and the youngest and possibly the most tender, he was afraid for his own safety. The following story has been passed down in the Hayman family:

> They supposedly, after starvation was looming, drew lots as to the first one to be sacrificed for the good of the rest. The man was given a several rod [16.5 feet – originally defined as the total length of the

left feet of the first 16 men to leave church on a Sunday morning] head start and while the rest were chasing him found the herd of wild hogs.

Realizing that they need not resort to cannibalism, they tried to stop the young man's flight but, gripped with fear, he tried to jump a gorge and fell into the river. He was swept out to sea. This was never mentioned in the inquest, for obvious reasons.[10]

Fact or fiction? There is no river on the Auckland Islands that could sweep a man out to sea. However, someone running in panic, looking over their shoulder, stumbling over rocks, could have easily fallen over one of the deep narrow indentations into the sea. It is a strange and horrible story, apparently too horrible to make up, but the truth will never be known. Teer said almost nothing about personal interactions in the group, though one of Hayman's descendants recalled that Mary Ann Jewell 'was elected governess of the island to quell the unrest because of the conditions'.

As would be expected, the presence of one woman caused some sexual tension. Most of the men, however, respected her, with one exception, as Keith Eunson notes in his account of the shipwreck. According to his nephew John Fegan, Irish passenger Patrick Caughey was said to have 'at times showed an alarming interest in Mrs. Jewell'. On one occasion, too, crewman Billy Scott 'made an insulting remark to Mary Jewell . . . and when tackled about it by Teer adopted so truculent an attitude that a fight ensued. Although Scott was a nuggety character, he was no match for the bull-like strength of Teer and was smashed to the ground with a powerful punch to the head.'[11]

It is difficult not to speculate what the survivors knew of the cargo. Certainly, the first officer would have had full knowledge of the gold on the manifest, and any other gold aboard; and, if the later rumours are true, so did William Sanguilly. No mention was ever made of trips to the west coast: indeed Sanguilly testified that none had been made. The survivors were on the island for almost two years. They braved the trip back and forth to Carnley Harbour, albeit in the lee of the island, so is it not unreasonable to think that sheer curiosity may have taken them around the west coast to the site of the wreck? If the wreck is as far south as many think, then it is more likely the men at Carnley Harbour would have gone. On the other hand, common sense may have ruled, for if they lost their boat they would be stranded. Then again, the others knew where they were, so it might have been worth taking the chance.

Chapter 8

Rescue Mission

On 25 January 1868 Captain Paddy Gilroy, with Henry Armstrong, representing the Southland Provincial Government, pointed the *Amherst* south once again. Their mission was to search for castaways: they were hoping against hope to find the four who had left for New Zealand so many months before. They stopped first at Stewart Island to capture weka to be released on the southern islands, then proceeded to the Snares, 65 miles away. Captain George Vancouver had described these as 'a cluster of seven craggy islands'.[1] The largest is just a mile and a half wide, with only one tiny sheltered bay in which a small ship could shelter in good conditions. Armstrong's report recounted what they found.

> Thousands of mutton-birds, nellies, penguins, etc heralded our approach, and to some extent prepared us for what we saw on landing. Once on shore our party was divided, and we commenced our search. I and two others made for the west side, where we climbed a high bluff, some 500 feet high, commanding a good view of the whole island. Our progress was painfully slow, the entire surface being literally honey-combed with mutton-bird holes, into which the foot sank deeply at every step, the inmates there-of betokening their dissatisfaction at our presence by giving vent to half-choked querulous cry. The penguins (ludicrous birds) in hundred, drawn up in rank and file, stood to oppose us on our march, and it required not a little vigorous kicking to force our way through them.

Despite firing the grass in the open and making 'a considerable smoke', during their four-hour stay they found 'no evidence whatever to show that any one was or had been living on the island', and returned to their boat. The other search party joined them 'with a like report'.

Before leaving we erected on the rocks at the point a large pole 15 feet long, on which are secured two bottles; one containing a letter notifying our visit, and for what purpose. The other filled with matches (well wrapped up in flannel), fish-hooks, a knife, and some dressed flax.[2]

On reaching the Aucklands, they set up the first depot in one of the huts on Enderby Island. In it they placed a case containing blankets, compass, matches, tools and other items. Armstrong wrote the message on the case which has become legend: 'The curse of the widow and fatherless light upon the man who breaks open this box, whilst he has a ship at his back'. A March newspaper article about the *Amherst*'s expedition supported this admonition:

It may be said that deposits of this kind will be exposed to depredation. We believe, however, few seamen would consider this misappropriation as less than sacrilege. They might well apprehend the hour when in the distress brought upon them by calamity, there would be neither pity or help; that an avenging power would pursue them, and that in the agonies of their desolation they would be tortured by a remorse which nothing could remove.[3]

Armstrong backed up his famous cautionary words with a letter dated 1 February 1868, signed by him on behalf of the Southland government and sealed in a bottle.

Brig *Amherst* (Captain Gilroy) chartered by the Government of Southland for the purpose of forming depots of necessaries for castaways on the Auckland and Campbell Islands, and of searching on these, the Antipodes and Bounty Islands for survivors from wrecks.

There have been left here today by order of the Government of Southland, a case (hermetically sealed) containing absolute necessaries for the use of castaways. I need not add *exclusively* for their use, for surely no one with a ship at his back will have so little respect for his manhood as to take aught of what is contained in this box. Three similar depots will be made in other parts of the island. One at Port Ross, one at the head of Saddle Hill Inlet (third bay south from this), and another in Carnley Harbor (the Straits).

Those who may come after, I will ask, in the name of suffering humanity, to see that the cases are preserved from injury and that the landmarks remain firm in their places. Should the lettering on the boards be indistinct, pray renew with paint. Two wood hens (wingless species) of opposite sexes have been turned into the scrub. These birds should not be molested for a few years until their number is considerably increased. Visitors to the Islands are therefore earnestly requested to extend their protection to them For the benefit of castaways, be it known that the mutton-bird burrows in the ground (like the sand martin), and both young and old can be easily secured by introducing the hand into the hole. They are excellent eating. The albatross and other sea birds lay their eggs on the high land.

The course from a point half a mile to the north of Enderby's Island to South Cape, Stewart's Island is north ¼ west, 198 miles. When you have read this please return rolled up into the bottle and cork securely.[4]

Along the front of the hut, under the eaves, they 'nailed firmly' a 16-foot board, painted white, on which was carved 'in deeply cut letters, four inches long, "Depot of necessaries for castaways, Landed from the brig *Amherst*, Feb. 1st, 1868. By order of the Government of Southland."'

The searchers then set off for the west coast to see if there was any wreckage left from the *General Grant*. They departed at daybreak in two five-oared whaleboats, one commanded by an officer, the other containing Gilroy and Armstrong. As they rounded the North West Cape they were met by a strong south-easterly wind 'sweeping down the gullies with fearful violence, lashing the water into spray, and at times almost turning the boats round'.

We pulled along the foot of the cliffs down to the entrance of the straits, never further from the rocks than three hundred yards and occasionally, when doubling a point, only fifty or sixty, scanning carefully every gully and every cave, but we saw nothing even approximating to the description given by the *General Grant*'s people of the cavern into which their ship drew.

At a point on the coast from which Disappointment Island bore N.W., we observed lying on a shelf of rocks and on a beach at the foot of the cliffs, some spars and fragment of wreck. Near these places a little to the south is a gulch, formed by two great masses of rock jutting out into the sea, (like buttresses) between which we believe the

ship to have jammed herself in. Whether our imaginations helped us
or not I can't say, but we fancied the rocks above appeared marked by
the vessel's masts; some fractures looking fresh. Moreover, the water
shoaled here.

It would be, however, impossible for any save those who escaped
from the ship, to point to the exact place where she drove in, there
being so many of these gulches and all so much alike in appearance.

No wreck was seen further than what I have already mentioned,
and prudence forbade our lingering to make a closer search, the hour
being late, and the weather looking 'dirty'. We noticed several places
where a landing could be effected in tolerably fine weather; one spot,
indeed, where a boat might be hauled up (by practiced hands).[5]

Like others before and after him, Henry Armstrong was awestruck by
the Aucklands. 'What can I say of this coast but that I have seen nothing
to surpass, or even equal, the grandeur, the savage majesty of its grim
storm-beaten sea walls; standing up bold and defiant, sullenly challenging
old Ocean to a trial of strength.' He noted the portions where 'the cliffs
rise perpendicularly to a height of nearly 500 feet, their sides presenting
a perfectly plane surface, at their feet a small shelf of rocks, or a long, low
cavern; the sea breaking over the one, and driving into the other with a
noise as of distant thunder'.

A newspaper article on 5 March 1868 praised the *Amherst*'s trip and
the leaving of castaway depots:

> not only was all left that could be left for the relief of any future
> sufferers, but provision was made for their instruction and
> consolation by depositing copies of the Holy Scriptures and other
> religious books, in popular esteem. These are acts worthy of record;
> not to be rewarded with gold and silver as their highest recognition,
> but claiming the warm approbation of society. Such deeds ennoble
> the maritime profession and render the name of a British seaman
> respectable in the eyes of the world.

The columnist also touched on wider matters raised by the loss of the
General Grant:

> The touching appeal of the survivors to the Governments of these
> colonies, will, we are sure, not be wholly disregarded. What it is
> possible to do can only be defined by practical men. It may often

happen that a philanthropic impulse based upon an incomplete view of facts, cannot be obeyed. But undoubtedly we are bound, considering the extent of commerce and its constant growth, to have regard to all means possible to mitigate the miseries of shipwreck. . . . The lesson of the *General Grant* may well be added to many others recorded in nautical memoirs of the result of calm, quiet effort, and reliance upon the aid which is generally attained by all who aid themselves.[6]

Part Two

Dreamers, Schemers and Divers

The *General Grant* was waiting.
Eroded in a sub-Antarctic cave,
the seas, her bones have sucked and scarified.
She beckons only the foolish or the brave.

Jack Duggan

The story never rests. It's not just historians who have written about it. It has attracted poets, playwrights, novelists and story-tellers. There are at least five novels (including one in French), a children's book, a folk ballad and many poems.

Of all the fanciful claims that have been made about the *General Grant* and its gold, surely the most bizarre is that made by Raymond Lamont Brown in his book, *Phantoms, Legends, Customs and Superstitions of the Sea*: 'For several nights previous to her wrecking, the *General Grant* had been followed by a mystery ship: many on board believed that their pursuer was the *Flying Dutchman*.'

But it is a fact that in a pub in Scotland, a posh club in England or around an open fire in New Zealand, someone may still say, 'If I had the money, this is where I'd tell you to search for the *General Grant*.' Those who have hunted for the wreck and its treasure are bound together by the mystique of tales of holds filled with gold, castaways, towering cliffs and lost caves. It is on a vessel heading southward – one hand for yourself, the other for the maps, notes, pencils sliding back and forth on the table – that you feel the heart and soul of the *General Grant*. The old-timers tell the story yet again to the uninitiated, and so more are brought into the circle of dreams.

Chapter 9

Tempting Fate

Over the next eight years, three survivors, James Teer, David Ashworth and Cornelius Drew, went back to the Aucklands to search for the gold. Only two returned. It was obvious that anyone going down to try to find the *General Grant* would wish to have an eyewitness to point out the cave, but these guides proved of very little use: expeditions with survivors seemed to spend just as much time as others ranging fruitlessly up and down the coast.

Within days of arriving back in New Zealand, James Teer was approached by two unidentified Southland brothers from Bluff,[1] who proposed that he guide them to the location of the wreck. When the ship went down Teer had lost his money belt containing 300 gold sovereigns so he was more than willing to accept the offer.

The ownership and background of the 87-ton paddle wheel tug *Southland*, which was to take Teer, Captain John Kirkpatrick, a diver named Putwain and a crewman named Rowe are murky. It is not known whether the two brothers remained in the picture or whether funding came from other backers, with Kirkpatrick and Teer as front men. The tubby little *Southland* was a relatively new ship, built in 1864 for the Southland Provincial Council as a harbour tug for Bluff. Her design was not a great success and after a short trial she was sold. There were two listings for her ownership in 1867: John Parkin Taylor, Superintendent of Southland Province, and West Coast merchant James Spence from Hokitika. It is likely that Teer's later connection with and residence on the Coast came through Spence.

The *Southland* left Westport on 28 February 1868 and after a brief stop at Hokitika arrived in Bluff on 3 March 1868 to collect James Teer. On Friday 6 March (according to his diary), Captain Kirkpatrick sent a telegram to the Spence brothers in Hokitika. It may be that they were not just the owners of the vessel, but also the backers of the venture.

On Sunday, 7 March 1868, Captain Kirkpatrick, James Teer, Putwain the expedition diver and the rest of the crew of 18 boarded the *Southland*. It was, as an account by Putwain, published in the *Southland News*, recounted,

> a wild day on shore even, and there was some talk of postponing our departure. But our captain was not of the yielding sort, and about noon he gave the order to cast off, and we slowly steamed away from the crowd of friendly faces which had assembled on the wharf to wish us God speed. When we got to outside, we found that our first experiences in the Southern Ocean were not to be peaceful, for the wind was dead in our teeth, blowing more than an old salt's half-gale, and we had besides a heavy head sea to contend with.[2]

On 2 May 1868, a battered little ship, missing stanchions, bulwarks, part of the starboard paddle box and its boat, limped into Bluff after struggling home through a wild storm, and the story spread of storm, frustration and failure.

The wild weather had forced them to take 10 days nipping in and out of harbours along the coast of Stewart Island and it was not until the 14th that they were able to make the run down to the Aucklands, finally anchoring in Port Ross on 22 March. They then had to sit out 'one continuous gale with hail and sleet' until the 29th when at last they woke to calmer seas and they were able to get an early start for the west side of the island. 'At 11 am the steamer was abreast of the place indicated by Mr. Teer as where the *General Grant* was wrecked.'[3]

When Putwain first saw the site he was 'very much deceived, or, if I may use the word, disappointed with its appearance. I had expected to see a huge, dark cavity, big enough to entomb the Great Eastern. Instead of this, I was met by a place which looked hardly big enough for our long boat to sail into with her sails set.'[4] The *Southland* stood off the cliffs, as the crew let down the lifeboat, for Putwain and Teer to try to make their way into the cave.

> We found on nearing the rock, however, that the wash was too strong to trifle with, and we therefore stood out to the center, and pulled in from there. Every stroke we took now we found the wash of the

sea was getting stronger, and as we advanced it was with the greatest difficulty our oarsmen could keep their seats.

All this while I had my eyes fixed on the cave, and I could not for the life of me make out how a ship of the size of the General Grant had found her way into it in the manner generally described.

When we were about 100 yards from the entrance of the cave, the men found that they could no longer keep their oars in the rowlocks, and the officer in charge did not think it prudent to go any further. However, we were far enough now for all good purposes, and I proceeded to take a good look at the cave.

As we came within the influence of the wash, as we passed under the shadow of the black, overhanging deadly cliff, not a sound was heard from any of us, and the hushed voice of our brave captain as he passed his orders to the engineers seemed to impress us all with its solemnity.[5]

The boat was hoisted on board and the steamer backed in slowly and carefully, taking soundings as she approached the shore, the water gradually shoaling from 25 fathoms (which was the least water obtained). When the steamer was about forty yards from the rocks, and 200 from the spot where the vessel sank, the rebound of the waves against the rocks suggested that it was not prudent to venture any further in. Captain Kirkpatrick described this part of the coast as 'cliffs rising perpendicularly out of the sea', and for a distance of twenty miles he saw only one place where it appeared possible that a man might climb to the top from the sea.

The gulch where the *General Grant* was lost has a compass bearing south-west by south from Disappointment Island, at a distance of eight miles. It forms a deep indentation in the cliffs and is about 300 yards wide at the mouth and gradually slopes inwards until it forms a large cavern running underneath the cliffs. At 1 pm the *Southland* steamed away, and anchored in North Harbour.[6]

Stopped only by the backwash from the cave, they were convinced that if they waited until the storm swell abated they would be able to go in, make their dives, recover the gold and return to Bluff in triumph. 'Light of heart and having forgotten all about the sleeping dead', they anchored in North Harbour and prepared their diving apparatus for the next day. But daylight brought a maddening, howling, raging gale. A gale which lasted without intermission from that day till, a month afterwards, we in despair sailed away from Sarah's Bosom in the midst of a hurricane which nearly blew us out of the water, but which, like a brave man as he is, our captain faced and weathered.

How we would have got through that month, if it had not been that we were buoyed up by a never dying hope that the next day would bring a change in the weather, I don't know.[7]

They anchored for five days in North Harbour before moving on to Port Ross, then headed south along the east coast with the idea that they could approach the suspected wreck site from a closer anchorage in Carnley Harbour. However, the weather changed once again. On 9 April they made another fruitless attempt to reach the wreck site by ship through Victoria Passage and northward up the west coast.

Totally frustrated by weather, they thought there might be a possibility of rigging up a platform from the top of the cliff and operating the diving bell from that. Kirkpatrick, Rowe, Putwain and the engineer made their way to the top of the cliffs above the cave. Putwain did not describe this brutal hike but it was no jaunty walk up a hill. They would have made their way through dense rata forest – that ironwood which did not bend but wrapped around itself, creating almost impenetrable walls so that they had to get around or crawl under the leaning trunks, lying flat and wriggling along seal tracks. As the slope became steeper, rough, muddy, rocky clearings, where the land had given away and slid down, provided a respite from the clinging, unyielding branches. Between these 'slip slopes' were rock cliffs hidden behind screens of myrsine, ready to trap the unwary. It was simply impossible to go through this scrub – the only way was to go around it, or roll over the top. Finally, they would have reached the level where the only remains of ground cover was enormous, cutting clumps of poa grass set three or four feet apart, and interspersed with black sticky bogs. The four men did well to accomplish this in four to five hours.

The result, however, was just one more disappointment:

One look at the sea beating below was enough to satisfy us that any attempt to rescue the gold of the General Grant must be made from seaward. While here, we amused ourselves throwing boulders into the ravines, which in many places divided the hills. To hear them as they thundered through the air, and, as they fell, awoke a thousand slumbering echoes, which died away faintly in the distance, was worth nearly the journey down to the coast. Unfortunately, we had not a stopwatch with us, or we might have got at the exact height of the cliffs by this means.[8]

They had been on the islands for almost eight weeks and apart from the one close look at the cave they had accomplished nothing – Putwain had not had the opportunity of even one dive. According to Captain Kirkpatrick's diary, even though they were able to supplement their diet with potatoes and turnip tops (descendants of the vegetables left by the Enderby settlers), their stores ran low and they were forced to abandon their salvage attempts. As a final gesture before leaving Carnley Harbour, they pulled the diving boat onto the shore for the use of anyone who might need it, and headed the *Southland* for home.

A secondhand report by a crewman from the *Southland* in the *New Zealand Mail* of 31 August 1899 (some 31 years after the voyage) stated:

> We had used up all our coal and provisions and so we determined to make for Bluff Harbour, the nearest point in New Zealand. We had to get fuel for the furnaces somehow, so we killed a lot of seals which were plentiful on the island, and you never witnessed such a mess as when we came to cut them up and pass on the junks to the stoke-hole. I was supposed to be carpenter and to superintend all the cutting up business. We had to rake up all the old saws, hatchets, even spades and so forth to cut up the 'fuel'. It was a gory affair but what could we do? We could not stay there and starve. We could not exist on penguins and their eggs. But, mind you, both are very good eating if you bury them in the sand for four and twenty hours. Before we got to Bluff we had broken up all the cabin fittings and even the steamer's lining timbers for fuel. The *Northland* [*sic* – the names in the report were deliberately changed but are quite recognisable] was the old sort, a fearful swallower of coal or its substitutes.

According to Allan Eden, a coastwatcher stationed on the islands during the Second World War, 'It is believed that subsequent disputes amongst the personnel led to the attempt being abandoned.'[9] It would not be surprising that, after coping with such appalling weather and disappointment, men cloistered in a small space would become short-tempered. The islands, however, are known for long stretches of bad weather, and the group may simply have decided that, with two months of their stores gone, it was not worth staying any longer.

James Teer never made it back to Ireland; nor did he ever recover the gold for which he had worked so hard. After the failed expedition to the Aucklands he returned to the West Coast, where, wearing his sealskin clothes, he gave lectures about his castaway adventures. According to the *Dictionary of New Zealand Biography* (*DNZB*), Teer sold his notes about the *General Grant* to a number of salvage ventures.[10]

In 1874 Teer was earning a living as a boatman on the Hokitika River and the following year settled at Arawata, near Jackson Bay in South Westland. The *DNZB* states that he clashed with Duncan MacFarlane, the Resident Agent for Jackson's Bay Special Settlement, for killing seals, his favoured diet, out of season.[11]

In 1889 a Sydney newspaper reported that he had planned to go back to the Aucklands that year but had died in his bed in Melbourne the night before the expedition was due to leave. In fact Teer had died two years earlier on 30 April 1887. A letter from a neighbour published in the *West Coast Times* a month later recounted the sad details of his passing. Late one afternoon, while cutting wood, he felt unwell and sent for help. The neighbour found him crouching over his fire 'shivering as if in an ague fit and moaning heavily. He complained of pain in the lower part of his abdomen, and said he was suffering intense pain.' After he was put to bed with hot compresses his breathing became laboured and he complained of 'a great weight on his chest. Finally he appeared to go to sleep, and in three hours from the time he took ill he was dead.'[12] When he was buried in Arawata Cemetery on 3 May a mourner poured a bottle of whisky over the coffin, in a traditional West Coast sign of mateship and admiration. Unfortunately no traces of Teer's grave now remain but the West Coast Historical Museum in Hokitika has in its collection the sealskin hat he made on the Auckland Islands.

Following Teer's expedition with great interest was another survivor, David Ashworth, by now a prosperous businessman, having established his own asphalt business after his return to Australia. When Teer returned empty-handed, Ashworth and a Captain Wallace of Winter's Flat, Castlemaine, Victoria, formed a partnership to search for the gold and purchased, or perhaps chartered, a little 48-foot topsail schooner called the *Daphne*, a ship with an unfortunate history. With the opening up of agriculture in Queensland and Fiji a deplorable practice known as 'blackbirding' began – the recruitment and sometimes kidnapping of young Melanesians to work in the sugar-cane fields. Between 1863 and 1904, over 62,000 people from the Melanesian archipelagos were enticed onto European ships. The Polynesian Labourers Act allowed ships to 'recruit' a certain number of workers and bring them to Australia. The *Daphne* had a permit for 58, but was caught in 1868 carrying over 100 and again in 1869 with 108 aboard. Her owners were finally brought before the courts and after a long and convoluted lawsuit were acquitted. The fact that in January 1872 the *Daphne* was sighted on the western side of the northernmost island of the Torres Group,[13] back in the blackbirding trade after only two years, suggests that Ashworth and Wallace had only chartered the vessel.

It may seem strange that many of these expeditions set out in late autumn, or early winter, just when the weather would be at its worst, but these were businessmen, and since success at salvage was far from a certainty, they could always offset some of their costs by sealing. The *Daphne* expedition set off in March 1870 from New River, also called Oreti River, near Invercargill. On board were Wallace, Ashworth (acting as second mate), Joseph Moss (first mate), James Cossar (diver and carpenter), crewmen Frank Leinster and James (Jim) Bailey, Kanak seaman Robert Seeman, ship's boy Richard Boyd and cook James Cousins.

When about 75 miles from Port Ross, the *Daphne* was thrown on her beam ends by a squall but quickly righted. Nevertheless it took 13 days before they safely anchored in Port Ross. Their first act on arriving was to take down the main topmast and the foreyard. This had the dual purpose of reducing windage (resistance to the wind), making the vessel less vulnerable to sudden gusts of wind, and providing ridgepoles for shelters on shore or to make a block and tackle for moving the barrels of seal oil. Despite deteriorating weather, they spent the next seven weeks hunting seals.

Richard Boyd later stated that during one of the seal-hunting trips, they found, and buried, five skeletons. It was assumed, probably correctly, that these bodies were crew from the *Invercauld* who had made it ashore from the wreck and perished from starvation and cold. Boyd also reported that the stores in the Port Ross Provision Depot had been broken into and that the tinderbox, matches, fishhooks, powder and musket had been left exposed to the weather and were spoiled.

It was not until the end of the second week of May that they began to make preparations to explore the west coast for the *General Grant*. Once it was found, they planned to use the larger ship's boat to conduct the actual diving operations. Wallace, Moss, Ashworth, Cossar (diver and carpenter), Leinster and Bailey would take the 28-foot whaleboat, provisioned for a week with potatoes, meat, bread and biscuit, together with two fowling pieces (shotguns), powder and shot. They also took sheet lead and tacks in case the boat sprang a leak. They departed before dawn on 19 May, in fine weather, leaving Cousins, Boyd and Seeman behind in the relative protection of Laurie Harbour to start building the diving platform.

This trio carried on their daily tasks, waiting expectantly for the others to return. The day after they left the wind had picked up, but this was typical of the Auckland Islands. After a week, however, their fears grew as the boat did not reappear. The missing men were all experienced hands: Joseph Moss, the mate, was a well-known Stewart Island whaler and boatman. Putting aside their building, Cousins, Seeman and Boyd combed the shoreline, and waited for the call of their friends coming out of the bush. Silence. The terrifying realisation came that they were alone on the islands, without those who had the skill to get them home. For five long weeks they waited, afraid to sail the *Daphne* back to New Zealand with only three crew. They found a part of a ship's boat and an oar lying in the kelp but were unable to say conclusively that it came from the *Daphne's* boat. Finally they had no choice but to attempt the journey home.

When the *Daphne* limped into Invercargill after a 10-day voyage, the shock of the news of the lost men quickly grew into anger and accusations flew wildly when it was learnt that the six men had disappeared over five weeks before. What had Cousins, Boyd and Seeman been doing all that time? Surely, they must have realised after a couple of weeks that a shore search was insufficient. Why hadn't they sailed out to look for them? Why hadn't they checked the islands more fully? Why hadn't they come back sooner for help? But for two men and a boy to sail a 48-foot schooner along the west coast would have been foolhardy. Cousins, although reputedly a 'master mariner', was elderly, Boyd was just a youngster and Seeman was an inexperienced crewman.[14]

Writing of the *Daphne* expedition a century later, Raymond Lamont Brown says that following the *Daphne's* return to port, the crew reported that as they had lain at anchor 'a ghost ship [i.e. the *Flying Dutchman*] had appeared and bore down on them. Almost colliding, the phantom crossed the schooner's bows and then dissolved into a grey haze.'[15] This is from the writer who has the *General Grant* being wrecked on Disappointment Island, which he locates 'just south of the Marquesas'!

The sum of £200 was raised to refit the *Daphne* and send her back down with a full crew to search for the lost men. Captain Paddy Gilroy with Cousins and Captain Thomas Thomson, the harbourmaster from Bluff, set out on 11 July 1870. Once at the islands they found HMS *Blanche* searching for another ship and the two groups united their efforts, but to no avail. David Ashworth and his companions had become six more victims of the sinking of the *General Grant*.

One more survivor would risk returning to the islands. An Australian syndicate headed by Messrs Stevens and Taylor, who were backers of the expedition, persuaded *General Grant* castaway and crewman Cornelius Drew to join them on an expedition that left Sydney in the *Flora* on 1 July 1876 under the command of a Captain Sullivan with a crew of 15. The *North Otago Times* of 10 August 1876 reported that 'a member of Parliament at whose expense the vessel was fitted out, has gone with them to superintend operations'. The vessel carried a variety of equipment including diving suits, navvy's tools, an abundance of blasting powder and a litho-fracteur.

Since a seaward approach had so far failed, their strategy was to set up camp in Port Ross, then cut a track up and across the top to the west coast cliffs just above the wreck site, where they would build a work camp. It was not until the track was completed, after a month's hard work, that they realised that Port Ross was not suitable as a base so the camp was moved southward to Smith's Harbour and the whole process started again. This first attempt was above the site that Teer had chosen, but Drew disagreed with his location. They explored the coastline and put men over the cliff on ropes, but all they found was miscellaneous wreckage.

On hearing of this proposed expedition, Joseph Jewell, one of the *General Grant* survivors, wrote a letter to the Melbourne *Argus* which was reported in the *West Coast Times* of 10 August 1876. In it Jewell states:

The plan proposed by the expedition is to blast the face of the cliff down in front of the cave wherein the ship sank and so form a breakwater: then sink a shaft, with a view of reaching the wreck from the cliff above. But as it rises to a great height, and the water where the ship sank is 18 fathoms deep, deepening rapidly towards the mouth of the cave, it follows that it would take an immense quantity of material to form the break-water, besides taking a large amount of labour to sink the shaft. Then there is the probability of the wreck having slid towards the mouth of the cave. In that case the chances are that it would get buried in forming the breakwater.

Jewell goes on to say that the timing is wrong as 'there are only two months of the year when anything can be done on the coast, November and December, in consequence of the strong gales that prevail.' He finishes by recommending that 'a party of 10 men, including a couple of divers go down there and anchor in the nearest sheltered spot, occupy their time while waiting for a favourable chance to get at the wreck, in catching seals, which abound, and by this means defray the expenses of the expedition, if unsuccessful in recovering the 500,000 pounds worth of gold said to be in the *General Grant*'.

Stevens had hired an engineer and blasting expert who, after examining the area, decided that the best way to proceed was (as originally planned) to tunnel into the overhanging cliffs above the spot where the *General Grant* was wrecked and blow them down. To his way of thinking, the cliffs would fall outside the vessel and form a protecting wall behind which salvage operations could be carried out. This plan, however, was sabotaged by the Irish pilot, Con, who 'believed the vessel would be hopelessly buried beneath thousands of tons of rock if the engineer had his way, and while the others were elsewhere he heaved the explosives into the sea from the cliffs'.[16]

The *Flora* arrived back in Port Chambers on 10 October 1876. The shipping reporter of the *Otago Witness*, writing four days later, stated that the expedition had returned without success and that the *Flora* herself had narrowly escaped shipwreck and that the amount of gold on board the *General Grant* was 'a smaller quantity than is usually supposed'.

It is unfortunate that the readers of the *Southland Weekly News* of 19 May 1877 did not respond positively to a small article buried on page 5. If they had, we would have had a unique description of the Drew adventure.

A member of the late expedition of the recovery of the gold supposed to be still on board the *General Grant*, wrecked several years ago at the Auckland Islands, has sent us some 'lines' descriptive of his adventures. We did at first think of publishing them, but on reflection it occurred to us that it would be better just to give a sample, and wait until our readers made some sign of wishing to have the remainder. In accordance with this idea we quote the following:

> *'But the weather was bad, and the grub it got short,*
> *Before we quite found the cave that we sought.'*

Chapter 10

Mutiny and Murder Averted

In 1877 an expedition on the 47-ton SS *Gazelle* was organised under the names of Irishman Captain McConville and one Captain Giles. The exact roles played by the two men are unclear. Contemporary reports in the press were minimal and it was not until 1954 that more of the *Gazelle* expedition story was told.

It is known that before the *Gazelle* left for the Auckland Islands, a complete overhaul of the vessel was undertaken. At the time of the expedition, the vessel was owned by Hugh Percy Aynsley, a merchant of Lyttelton, New Zealand. It is unclear if Aynsley had any involvement with the expedition or whether the vessel was simply chartered from him. This expedition seems to have made two trips to the Auckland Islands. The first, which left early in 1877, reputedly included *General Grant* survivor Cornelius Drew and a diver called Dominique Farre. The *Gazelle* returned unexpectedly in early May to drop off Farre and Drew, recruit a new diver, G.H. Sherwill, re-provision and take on more coal. The *West Coast Times* of 10 May 1877 reported that Captain Giles had 'found the supposed wreck of the *General Grant* after severe exertions and risk in twelve fathoms of water. Diving operations are not begun. Mr Stevens and one man remained by the wreck. The captain feels confident of getting the gold on his return.'

On 4 June the *West Coast Times* reported that the SS *Gazelle* was to be sent back to the Auckland Islands without delay and that 'Captain McClutchie intends to form a company on a small scale for the purpose of recovering the gold in the wrecked ship *General Grant*'.

The *Gazelle* returned to the Aucklands on 13 July 1877. According to the *Southland News* of 14 July:

She takes four divers with her, and two diving dresses, so that in case of accident in this matter, they will rectify the same at the island. Altogether the expedition is better fitted out, and a long supply of provisions being taken, this trip will no doubt decide whether the gold is there, and should it be, we earnestly hope they may return amply rewarded for the risks and hardships the *Gazelle*'s crew must necessarily endure in searching for it.

Sherwill kept a diary and from his account it was not a happy ship. Once their base in Carnley Harbour was established, he was set to work exploring the coastline until they found a cave that fitted the earlier descriptions. There, he took soundings and reported that the water was 'so smooth and clear that he could see the bottom in seven fathoms' and was quite convinced that

> there is no trace of the wreck in the cave, as the two men and myself in the boat saw the bottom as clear as day. It is a rough stony bottom, where a ship would not last 24 hours in a gale of wind. The walls of the cave are about perpendicular at the entrance, and about 152 feet high by 64 feet wide for a distance of about 100 feet or more in, and then they close in to about 26 feet wide by 70 feet high. After this they open out to a great extent.[1]

Sherwill was an experienced diver: he had worked in the United States and had helped to salvage most of the cargo of the *Surat*. The *Surat* was a full-rigged ship which had been wrecked at the mouth of the Catlins River on the east coast of the South Island on 1 January 1874.

By mid-October, Sherwill had still not been given the order to dive and was thoroughly frustrated and angry. He had joined the expedition for treasure and he wanted to search for it, but for some reason the leaders hung back and the men sent to hunt for seals. On 31 October he wrote: 'It seems to me that we have a certain time to put in at the Auckland Islands, and until that time is up we will have to content ourselves where we are. As for the wreck of the *General Grant* it is hardly ever spoken of at all. Well, someone will have to pay for this, and I think it is my duty to send these memo [*sic*] to the papers.'[2] Sherwill's diary contains many complaints regarding the behaviour of Giles, the master of the *Gazelle*, and McConville, both of whom he felt would rather hunt seals or sit around drinking the brandy, which had been brought down for his use after diving, rather than actively search for the *General Grant*.

On 14 October the *Gazelle* again visited the west coast and found a quantity of ship's timbers, but none of these could be linked to the *General Grant*.

According to a 1955 article published in the *Southland Daily News* by F.W.G. Miller, at one point during the *Gazelle* expedition a party of crew members got lost in the bush and found the remains of a dead sailor lying by a rock that was inscribed 'George William Packer of London, fell overboard from the American barque *Iredera* 25 December 1875'. There was speculation that he had swum ashore only to starve to death. It was proposed that the men go back and give the body a decent burial but they were unable to find it again. There was then an altercation between the crew, in particular Sherwill, and Captain Giles, who was critical of them for wasting time on such a venture.[3] The *Gazelle* turned homeward on 17 November 1877 with a cargo of sealskins and reports of seeing wreckage of an unknown ship, but nothing else.

In 1954, when two new attempts to find the *General Grant* were reported as being planned, G.I. Moffet of Invercargill, whose family had had a lease on part of the Auckland Islands for farming purposes since the late 19th century, revealed to the *Southland Times* that he had Sherwill's diary in his possession and wanted the story to be published 'in the hope that the information it contains will discourage people from making any further fruitless attempts to find something that no longer exists'. The *Times* responded by publishing a scathing article about the *Gazelle* expedition and the role played by Captain McConville. In response McConville's son John, then 77, wrote to the paper to defend his father's reputation: 'This is the story told me by my father over 60 years ago, and I recount as well as my memory serves me without malice or intention to do harm or give offence to any person.'

> My father declared that the cave in which the General Grant was pounded to pieces was discovered, and the diver Sherwell [sic] endeavoured to get down, but with the diving gear of those days he could not submerge 50 fathoms – that is 300 feet. However, other attempts were made, using the ship's steward as diver, and although a portion of the wreck could be located, he also failed to reach the bottom. The terrific undertow in and out of the cave made it impossible to reach the wreck. Early in the expedition the leader sensed an undercurrent of unrest among the crew, and eventually one Dominque Farre confided to my father that, if successful in salvaging the gold, he (Captain McConville) was to be assassinated, the ship

seized by the crew and taken to a place where the gold would be divided, the ship scuttled and the crew dispersed.

John McConville explained that wooden railings from the *General Grant* were found in the cave, from which his father had carved a chess set that was in the Canterbury Museum.[4] He maintained, too, that Cornelius Drew was also on the *Gazelle* expedition, and he had confirmed that the wreckage recovered was from the *General Grant*'s bulwarks. James Higginson in his book *Yesterday's Gold* also maintained that Drew went back to the Auckland Islands a second time.[5] There is no other reference to Drew being on this expedition, but he may have confirmed the identity of the piece of wreckage after the *Gazelle* returned.

Over the years the Marine Department and its successor agencies have received numerous enquiries about the possibilities of salvaging the *General Grant*. In 1884 a John W. Douglas, of Charters Towers, Queensland, asked how much gold had been aboard. The reply discouraged any further attempts: 'A party went down to the Auckland Islands in the steamer *Gazelle* to endeavour to recover the gold about 7 or 8 years ago, but I understand that they could not even find the place where the wreck occurred'. No more was heard from this would-be treasure hunter.[6]

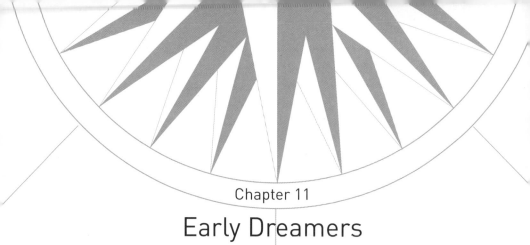

Chapter 11

Early Dreamers

We will never know how many ships and men have worked their way up and down the west coast of the Auckland Islands in search of the elusive cavern. It would be naive to think that ships did not slip out of Australian and New Zealand ports and make their way south. It is certainly possible that those on both legitimate and illegitimate sealing trips might have taken a day or two out just to have a look. The *Awarua*, owned by Joseph Hatch of Invercargill, was a regular visitor to the islands, for sealing, and for bringing supplies and animals to a farming venture there. Dr F.A. Monckton of Invercargill had a lease on the Auckland Islands from 1874 to 1877, but constant bad weather, the difficulty of getting farmhands and provisions, as well as stock, to and from the islands, meant that he forfeited his lease in 1877.

As James Higginson explains, 'The normal practice for ships working the southern oceans was to record their inwards and outwards movement in the Port Register at Bluff by their objectives, e.g. "sealing to the southern islands", or working the sealing islands. There are many such entries for the *Awarua* but at least two, written in the same hand as the others, merely list a bald destination – Auckland Islands – without any reason for the voyage.'[1]

On 4 July 1879 the *Awarua* landed seven men at Port Ross to go sealing: Charles Brown, Thomas Daley, William Chapman, G.M. Booze, J. Lawson, David Hunter and Charles Garnet. When the vessel returned in October with provisions neither the men nor the station whaleboat were there so, presumably believing them to be away sealing, the *Awarua* left for the Campbell Islands on 27 October. As the *Southland Times* reported on 21 February 1880, when another vessel called into Port Ross on 9 November, the provisions left by the *Awarua* were untouched, the presumption being that the men had gone round to the West Coast sealing and got their boat swamped. Had they succeeded, however, in getting safely to land, there would be no possibility of their getting away as the rocks are perpendicular, until some assistance was sent, but they might be able to exist on seal flesh, and would find shelter amongst the rocks and coves there.

But considering the well populated seal areas on offshore islands, and in Carnley Harbour, were the men really likely to have risked the west coast in search of seals? It is certainly possible, for seals were to be found on some rocky outcrops there, but it seems more likely that any trip to that area had an ulterior motive.

The *Awarua* was caught out in 1887 when she found the survivors of the *Derry Castle* while supposedly on an illegal sealing trip to the Aucklands. The *Derry Castle* was wrecked on Enderby Island and the eight survivors out of a total of 22 crew and one passenger spent four months on the islands before being rescued by the *Awarua*. The survivors were landed in Melbourne, but publicity about the rescue led to the master of the *Awarua* being prosecuted by the New Zealand authorities for illegal sealing.

The actual existence of the purported *Federal* expedition in 1887 is highly questionable for the only account found is in the 1923 prospectus of Marine Treasures Ltd. A man identified only as Captain B. (possibly a Captain Bryne) wrote the following for the company.

> I first visited the Auckland Islands in September, 1887, in the schooner Federal, 95 tons, with a crew of nine and diver, John Pattinson. He reported that the General Grant was lying in a cavity in 16 fathoms of water, but he could not get near enough to get on her deck, as the violence of the wash continually forced him in the direction of the rocks south of the wreck. The stumps of the main and mizzen masts were plainly visible to him and the vessel was lying with a list to port.[2]

In 1889 Hamilton N. Sleigh wrote to the Marine Department from the Grosvenor Club in New Bond Street, London.

Mr. Brandon of 62 Grey St Newcastle-on-Tyne and myself are proposing an attempt to recover the Treasure, but before taking active steps in the matter we are anxious to learn if it is necessary for us to obtain your authority and sanction and if so, to request you to grant us your permission for a given time, say until next March twelve months. Such sanction being granted will you inform us if any and what percentage on the net value of property found will be claimed by the Government of New Zealand.[3]

This request resulted in the first memorandum from the Solicitor General to the Minister of Marine about the due process to be undertaken by those wishing to search for the *General Grant*'s gold.

The powers and the duties of the Government depend on the facts. If this loss of the General Grant was a 'wreck' in legal acceptation and no owner can be found for the gold said to have been lost, then the Crown has certain rights. But if the owner is known then the Crown's rights do not arise, and the case is one simply of salvage and between each owner and the persons recovering the gold. Presumably it can be ascertained who was co-owner or co-insurer of the gold, and it would appear the best course for Mr. Sleigh is to ascertain all the facts before he starts his venture.[4]

And if ' active steps' were taken to recover the gold, the authorities in New Zealand would have to be given prior notice so they could ensure that ' the local law' was complied with. 'Of course this will not prejudice the rights of the owners of the gold, if they can be found.' The Solicitor General assumed that the *General Grant* was a British ship and therefore 'subject to the local law as to wrecks, salvage etc.'. When he was advised that she had in fact been an American vessel, he said that he did not think this made any substantial difference. Sleigh received a reply that was essentially the same as the one Douglas had been sent in 1884.

In 1893 a group described in a Sydney paper only as 'an Invercargill syndicate', 'failed to get a craft away'.[5] In 1895 another would-be salvor, John Aulsebrook of the famous biscuit and confectionery makers, Aulsebrook & Sons of Sydney, received a discouraging letter from New Zealand's Marine Department, explaining that a member of the *General Grant*'s crew 'was unable to fix the position of where the vessel was wrecked to within a mile. Nothing further is known than that it was on the west coast any place within 5 miles north east of

Bristow Point.'[6] Aulsebrook persisted, however: on 12 December 1896, he wrote to the Commissioner for Taxes and Customs in Wellington, asking for 'any information respecting the wreck of the Gen[l] Grant at the Auckland Isles in 1875 [*sic*] and any subsequent operations if any, to recover the £ 100,000 worth of gold in her. I quite well recollect the calamity but cannot just place following events.' He was asking because 'a clever man here, has all but perfected a Diving dress in which he alleges he can go almost any depth and has already proved this down to 440 feet. A prominent Gentleman [in the original the name was written, then heavily blanked out] & myself & another intend to prove it on the wreck of the "Cattecthum" presently & in the meanwhile ask for the above information anticipating your favors.' We do not know, however, if Aulsebrook ever mounted an expedition.

In 1903 the Minister of Marine was sent a clipping that began 'An American schooner has arrived in New Zealand with a party who propose to search for long-lost treasure' with a request on behalf of one of the survivors from the *General Grant* 'to inquire whether in the event of the treasure being found the prospectors will be at liberty to remove it'.[7] No more is recorded of this expedition, if indeed it ever existed.

A second expedition led by the mysterious Captain B supposedly took place in 1908. Once again, the only mention of it seems to be the Marine Treasures Ltd. Prospectus. This time the captain claimed to have 'charge of an expedition from 'Frisco to conduct salvage operations on one of the Pacific islands'. He had the 120-ton auxiliary schooner *Fearless*, with 11 crew and a diver called George Hamilton.

> The diver succeeded in getting a foothold on the deck of the *General Grant* after his fifth descent. He then reported her to be in 16 fathoms of water, fast on a submerged rock. He stated that masses of rock covered her in the same way, barring all possibility of access to the vessel's interior. The diver made two more descents with the object of trying to shift sufficient rock from the hatches to get into her hold, but, not having any dynamite and proper tackle, we were obliged to abandon this attempt.[8]

Since no reports can be found in the press, it is tempting to dismiss the accounts of this and the 1887 attempt as pure fiction, made up solely for the Marine Treasures prospectus, which was primarily intended to raise capital for a further expedition to raise the gold of the *General Grant*. It could be argued, however, that if the wreck had been found but the treasure not salvaged, Captain B was certainly not going to broadcast far and wide that the gold was there. Then again, anyone reading the survivors' accounts of the wreck could, with a little imagination, have created this expedition. As intriguing as they sound, without further evidence these must be regarded as phantom expeditions.

The next proposed expedition, in 1909, was to have featured the famous 204-ton New Zealand schooner *Huia*. Built by James Barbour at Aratapu, on the Wairoa River in Northland, she was launched in 1894 and made numerous voyages around the New Zealand coast, across the Tasman and to the Pacific Islands. After a long and illustrious career, the *Huia* was wrecked on Komekame Reef in New Caledonia in 1951. At the time of the proposed expedition she was owned by Kaipara mariner George McKenzie. Whether he had a financial interest in the expedition or was simply planning to charter his vessel is not known.

In November 1909 Stanley Chambers wrote to the Minister of Marine on behalf of the 'Huia Syndicate', explaining that 'the object of the enterprise [was] to go to the Auckland Is, with the schooner *Huia* to take a party of men and gear for the purpose of attempting to recover the lost treasure that went down in the *General Grant* in 1866'. He had already asked various insurance people but could find 'nobody financially interested in the *General Grant* treasure'. 'I have also written home to London to Lloyds to ask the position there. My Principals wish to know if the New Zealand Government. have any claim to this money. As a good deal of the time of the men will remain unoccupied from weather conditions the idea has been that they shall be employed in such spare time in sealing ...'[9] Nothing more was ever heard of Chambers or his syndicate.

In 1908 Captain Niels Sorensen, a Dane living in America who had formerly worked for the Auckland Harbour Board as a diver, entered the *General Grant* story. It was reported in the *Taranaki Herald* of 14 September 1908 that he had met one of the *General Grant* survivors 30 years before when he was oyster-digging in New Zealand. He proposed to sail from San Francisco to New Zealand, charter a special schooner and sail to the Auckland Islands from Dunedin.

'Now we are going to get that gold,' said Captain Sorensen. 'The New Zealand Government makes no claim to it. I have a concession permitting me to land a crew on the island. I shall doubtless find the hulk sound and strong. I shall have to blow out the side. To do this I will prepare a canvas hose, six inches in diameter, with loops along the side and will fill this with dynamite. When I go down after the flash, I will find a hole in the side of the hulk just under the captain's cabin and 20,000,000 dollars in gold bullion will be awaiting me. The gold is all packed in cases, each case valued at 5,000 dollars. The treasure can't sink in the mud, for it is hard sand and rock bottom.' The report went on to say that 'Captain Sorensen has had experience as a diver, and if the old ship is intact, he will have no difficulty in breaking through her timbers. He is at least very optimistic.'

In 1910 Sorensen wrote to the Marine Department claiming that a Mr White had lost $2 million worth of gold in the wreck: it had been stored in strongboxes under the captain's cabin. Sorensen also mentioned that a Mr Hargraves, the Chief Engineer of the Auckland Harbour Board Dredge, claimed that the *General Grant*'s chief officer, Bart Brown, was in fact alive and living in Christchurch under the name Watson. He had apparently 'never revealed his identity for fear of criminal punishment for negligence'. Sorensen listed the wrecks he had been involved in salvaging and stated that he had a sworn affidavit of having purchased the rights to the *General Grant* from an insurance company in Sydney in 1896, although the original copy of the document had been lost in a fire in New York in 1908. As evidence he supplied a copy of the document drawn up from memory.

On 17 January 1911, via secretary Bernard J. Isecke, the secretary of an Arizona company called the International Salvage Company (ISC) wrote to the New Zealand Prime Minister, Sir Joseph Ward, explaining that it had 'a right to and intend[ed] to salvage and recover the cargo of the ship *General Grant*'. Anxious, however, to operate 'in strict compliance with the laws of the Dominion of New Zealand', ISC asked 'respectfully' whether 'a lease can be obtained from your government of a certain part of the Isle of Auckland on the coast of which the ship *General Grant* was sunk, together with a right of entry to the island and the right to begin operations for the salvage and recover of the cargo of the ship'. Isecke stated that ISC claimed ownership of the ship and the gold 'by virtue of an agreement with Capt. N.C. Sorensen who in his turn obtained the right to salvage this ship and its cargo from the insurance companies who paid the loss of their successors'.

By now Captain Sorensen appears to have been in partnership with Eugene May, a businessman he had met in New York, and together they formed the May Sorensen Salvage Company. This rather confusing situation has come to light through correspondence in the New Zealand Marine Department file on the salvage of the *General Grant*. It would appear that Sorensen had sold his rights to ISC and yet was planning his own attempt in conjunction with May at the same time. ISC was anxious to know what its rights were if 'we succeed in the recovery of the cargo assuming that we were unable to obtain a duplicate assignment or otherwise to establish our ownership. In other words, we would like to know in that event what percentage of the recovery we would be entitled to under the Shipping and Seamen Act of 1908.' Isecke asked politely for 'a pamphlet copy of the act or acts relative to salvaging ships in your jurisdiction'.

The May-Sorensen syndicate reputedly had a capital of £30,000 and planned to spend about £10,000 on the expedition. The value of the gold that they planned to recover was between £300,000 and £400,000.[10] They planned to attack the wreck from the top of the cliffs by constructing a cantilevered platform. This was an incredibly ambitious project. It was one thing to sail a boat around to the west coast, running for cover when necessary, and in decent weather put down a diver; it was quite another to carry everything that was needed across the rugged terrain of the top of the island. The syndicate was granted a temporary year-to-year licence to make a chain-wide road from Port Ross to the site of the wreck 'and a 2 chain Reserve along [the] coast of the Island . . . for the purpose of using the land in connection with the salvage of the *General Grant*'.[11]

In 1912 the May-Sorensen syndicate bought the 49-ton steamer *Wairoa*, registered in Auckland, and brought her to Port Chalmers for fitting out. She was to be commanded by a Captain Perriam of England, 'who was familiar with the wreck-site'. There is some conflict, however, about the composition of the crew on this expedition. The *Truth* of 10 November 1954 quoted an old shipwright, Frank Agnew of Port Chalmers, who worked on the *Wairoa* refit. He said that the captain was John May, 'a slick-talking, quick-thinking Yankee . . . . What he was Captain of remained one of the unsolved mysteries of the expedition. His profound ignorance of seamanship was matched only by his knowledge of the art of share-pushing.' It is quite likely therefore that 'Eugene' and 'John' May were one and the same man and that Agnew had remembered the name incorrectly. At this point, May increased the cost of the proposed expedition to £15,000 but added that the value of the gold was now £500,000. The expedition even purchased bullocks in

Heriot for doing the heavy hauling once they reached the Aucklands and three men from Roxburgh were to accompany them as bullockies.

But the May-Sorensen syndicate ran into financial problems just as the *Wairoa* was ready to sail on 13 May 1912. A bailiff from Dunedin arrived at Port Chalmers at 3 pm, accompanied by a number of creditors, and nailed a writ to the mast seizing the vessel for debt for the repairs undertaken by Stevenson & Cook of Port Chalmers and other creditors.

In the general confusion May, having 'discovered that he had pressing business elsewhere', slipped away and took an early train to Invercargill. At the port in Bluff he was met at the gangway of an outward-bound ship and reminded of his debts. He managed, however, to leave New Zealand for Sydney, where he met up with his wife and daughters and headed back to San Francisco. The *Wairoa* was promptly sold by Stevenson & Cook to recoup their losses. The vessel and her stores raised £3,500, which satisfied some but not all of her creditors.[12]

May, however, was not beaten. He formed a new venture, the American Deep Sea Exploring Company, and the next year, 1913, he wrote from the States to say that he 'was leaving 'Frisco shortly with a schooner fully equipped in order to salvage the *General Grant*'. May reported that he had recruited a Captain Miller as his salvage expert and that his engineer for the expedition had been in contact with Cornelius Drew over a period of four years, who had pointed out the exact location of the wreck. May was informed by the New Zealand Marine Department that unless he commenced work by July 1914, his salvage licence would be cancelled. His syndicate was therefore reorganised and his licence was extended until October 1914, but that was to be the last extension as another applicant was seeking it. But May's vessel, the *Robert Henry*, was wrecked in American waters and the expedition's plans collapsed. The last we hear of May is an interesting reference to him in government correspondence saying that the writer could find no record of 'the statement that Mr. May has a contract with the New Zealand Government with regard to the manufacture of paper from cactus'.[13]

Many years later, in 1954, Hastings man W. H. Parker, who was to have accompanied the May-Sorensen expedition, told the local paper that 'a diver had unsuccessfully explored the seabed at the scene of the *General Grant*'s wreck'. He had spoken to the diver, a man named Mennan, in Dunedin shortly after the First World War. Mennan had told him 'that he had found only a few heavy timbers, probably part of the keel of the wrecked vessel. The remainder had obviously broken up, and had been scattered by turbulent currents, so that recovery of the main bullion – two small cases of gold – would be extremely difficult.'[14]

There was a flurry of correspondence in December 1913 and January 1914 with regard to an enquiry from Dunedin. 'Recently the Minister of Marine received a communication from a gentleman, whose name so far as could be made out from his signature, appeared to be J. Sawell. The address given was as 3 Maclaggan St., Dunedin. ... A reply was sent to him under the name of J. Sawell, but it has been returned as unclaimed...'. The elusive correspondent turned out to be a Mr Sowell, an employee of the accountancy firm Scoullar & Chisholm. He had written to ask the government to relinquish its usual claim on any booty found because of the expense which the Dunedin company had already undertaken. Sowell appears not to have had any official backing from his employer and was presumably writing on behalf of a private syndicate planning a salvage attempt. It seems likely that he added his employer's name to give credibility to his case.[15]

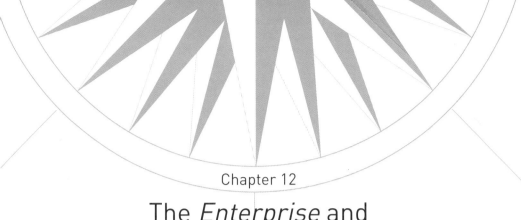

Chapter 12

The *Enterprise* and More Dreamers

Of the early salvage expeditions the most deserving of success was arguably that of the *Enterprise* over 1915 and 1916. After the failure of the May–Sorensen expedition planned during the period 1910 to 1913, the *General Grant* licence was put up for auction and bought by a firm of general merchants and engineers from Sydney headed by Percy Vincent Catling, a Londoner by birth, but living in Sydney. They bought a 24-ton oyster boat, the cutter *Enterprise*, which had been built in Halfmoon Bay, Stewart Island in 1883. The plan was to make two trips: a preliminary voyage in 1915 to survey the area and a second working voyage the following year to recover the gold.

Catling arranged to have two collector's edition stamps printed for fundraising purposes. The stamps are called 'cinderellas' or 'local stamps' by philatelists and although they are not official, they are highly prized because of the exotic locations from which they often originate. These stamps are now extremely rare: it is thought that only four or five covers are still in existence. In an Australian auction in September 2001, a block of four stamps of the 1915 halfpenny green and penny red Auckland Islands *General Grant* expedition cinderellas sold for $A60,287. Individual stamps from this expedition are still procurable through philatelic dealers at about $NZ100 each.

The 1915 trip almost ended in disaster before it even started. Two of Catling's crew, the diver Paul Suveran (a French-born naturalised British subject) and another man (named 'Atherton' in the 1954 'Wide World' magazine article, though his real name remains a mystery), arrived in New Zealand to join the expedition, bringing with them some diving equipment that Suveran had bought in London. However, a zealous customs inspector discovered that they had tried to smuggle Catling's rifle into New Zealand by concealing it in the false bottom of a crate. They were fined £25 or 28 days in prison. Unable to pay the fine, both men were jailed. To add insult to injury, all the equipment they had brought from London was impounded, and when it was sold at auction they had to try to buy it back. This they could not afford to do, and they were successful in purchasing only the diving suit, air compressors and some sundry diving equipment. Gone for good were their travelling trunks, charts, kerosene lamps and woolly underwear.

'Atherton' had been married shortly before leaving England and his wife accompanied him to New Zealand. While preparing for the expedition, his visits to the *Enterprise* became less frequent and eventually he pulled out of the venture. Frequent visits to the haunts of seafarers led to Catling recruiting Mathias Jorgen (Jack) Olsen, a Swede living in Port Chambers.

The *Enterprise* cast off from Port Chalmers near the end of June 1915, with Catling, Suveran and Jack Olsen on board. As they were leaving harbour their engine failed and they nearly collided with an incoming ship. When they finally got away, Suveran fell overboard on the first night and was rescued only because he was able to hang onto the rope that had caught around his leg. Catling noticed the phosphorescence created by the diver's movements in the water and hauled him back on board. Bad weather caused a further two-week delay and they were forced to shelter in Port Pegasus on Stewart Island.[1]

When they finally reached the Aucklands, their mainsail was in shreds and another wait ensued while it was being repaired. During this time they attempted to use their centreboard canoe to explore the coast but again bad weather delayed them. It was, after all, now the beginning of July – midwinter in these latitudes. Reputedly using Teer's notes (although how they obtained them is a mystery, as Teer had died 28 years before in 1887), they finally began serious exploration on 10 July. Catling decided to use Carnley Harbour as a base, as Captain McConville had done on the *Gazelle* expedition in 1877. They were searching for a deep indentation in the cliffs about 300 yards wide, gradually sloping inland until it formed a large cavern running underneath the cliffs. Three caverns in the area had been described as bearing south-west by south from Disappointment Island at a distance of eight miles. One cavern had collapsed, apparently quite recently, and if this had been the *General Grant* cave, any traces of the wreck were now buried for all time under tons of boulders. Catling, having narrowed down the possible location of the wreck, was still optimistic.

At this point they returned to Dunedin, after an absence of three months, to prepare for the main diving expedition. As an unidentified newspaper article sent to the Marine Department in July 1916 explained, the *Enterprise* was 'thoroughly fitted out for the arduous expedition'. Fitted with a new 14-horsepower engine, she carried stores for six months, 'an up-to-date diving plant, with special compressors and receivers; a dynamo and submarine electric lamps for night working, if found necessary; a telephone apparatus, to enable the diver to have constant communication with the surface', plus a four-horsepower launch, the *May Queen*, and two small boats.[2]

Captain Catling and a crew of four (including Olsen, E.P. Mennan and an unidentified cook) left Dunedin on 29 February 1916. After a short stay in Bluff, they departed south. On reaching the Auckland Islands, they made their base in Carnley Harbour. On 16 March they put the launch overboard and fitted her engine. Two days later, the *May Queen* left the harbour's western entrance on a strong flood tide. Despite thick fog, the launch was able to steam close inshore past Cape Lovitt, Bristow Point and the Great Rift. She began soundings in three of the bights, 'but the spike was too coarse and the water too thick for the observation telescope. Besides, the roll of the launch made things too jumpy for successful observation of the floor of the sea.' They had gone as far as the 'Red Rock' inside 'Beehive Bight', and almost reached the 'Great Arch' (these are Catling's names for various local geographical features, which have not survived on modern maps), when they decided to return 'to make a lead-weight, with silver-steel point, and also to improve the observation apparatus'. A gale was also rising, which forced the launch to return to the *Enterprise*. In the meantime they would work onshore 'and pick up the marks of the S.S. *Gazelle* expedition from the cliffs, and so ascertain the exact spot more quickly than by soundings'.[3]

They moved the *Enterprise* to Smith Harbour, but it was to be another two days before they were able to begin the hike to the tops via an old sealers' track. Following this, they

succeeded in penetrating to the west coast shortly before noon. After lunch they scaled the mountain which rears its head above the cove, after a painful climb over tussock interlaced with scrub. It was slow progress, and they were all dead beat when they reached it. They succeeded in making all the necessary observations, and also took several photographs which were considered essential. They had a terrific job getting back in their tired condition, and this was intensified by their missing the track. Many times they found themselves in bog well over the knees and they only covered 1¼ miles in 2½ hours.[4]

For six weeks after this, 'it blew a howling gale, the wind veering from the north-west to south-west. . . . Huge masses of water were being hurled into the western entrance, but the little *Enterprise* lay safe in her land-locked harbour. In an attempt, however, to secure a photograph of the swirling, heaped-up water, Captain Catling nearly lost his life.' The seas were breaking 60 feet up the cliffs at the harbour's western entrance. Nevertheless, they kept trying to get out to the coast, and on one occasion the launch was very nearly swamped and the motor flooded. 'A north-west hurricane swept over the Aucklands, and it was an act of Providence that the launch and all hands were not lost outside Carnley Harbour.'[5]

Catling and his men obviously knew the schedule of the *Amokura* which was due to visit the Auckland Islands. The NZS *Amokura* was a New Zealand Government training ship for seafarers, which regularly visited the subantarctic islands to replenish the provision depots and to search for castaways. When the gale had subsided, they took the launch to Camp Cove Depot and left mail and some money with a note that they would appreciate some fresh vegetables if the *Amokura* had any to spare. Perhaps because of a shortage of money, the expedition incorporated some of the local wildlife into their diet. Jack Olsen described their diet as 'Stewed seal, Roast Seal, Boiled seal, Boiled duck, Roast Duck and Seal and Duck Soup'.[6]

It was not until 18 May that the expedition was able to fossick outside the supposed wreck-site 'and even then there was a heavy swell that meant risk'. After weeks of inaction, however, they were keen to continue their search. With Olsen and Mennan, Catling set off in the *May Queen*, carrying all the sounding gear and observation apparatus. When they reached *General Grant* Cove at 12.30pm, they immediately started sounding. 'They tried all along the ledge (or buttress), and then crosswise over the cove. They next sounded along the opposite buttress, in front of the isolated ledge, and all round the sunken rock mentioned by the *General Grant* survivors.' It was while they were going over this rock that the men 'had a narrow escape of losing their lives'.

Although it had 8ft of water over it, two heavy rollers came in, and the first of them showed the rock quite close to the surface, and only about 2ft astern of the launch. The second roller was a tremendous one which broke, and in the hollow they saw the rock quite bare and only about 8ft astern of them. Captain Catling estimates that had the wave come, say, half a minute earlier, the bottom of the launch would have been smashed like an eggshell and that would have been the last of the expedition.

Fifty years to the day since the *General Grant* was wrecked, the *Enterprise* stood off the mouth of a cave which Catling believed had hidden the treasure for half a century.

> The *Enterprise* was brought round, and 700 fathoms of rope and two big anchors were put down. By means of these moorings the party were able to pull the vessel to and fro over the cove at the entrance to the cavern, and Captain Catling was able to go under and thoroughly examine the bottom. The weather was fine, and the vessel lay outside the cavern all that night. The crew saw the same overhanging masses of rock that the poor men on the *General Grant* had looked on 50 years before when their ship drove to destruction. Beetling rocks rose 650 ft., in many cases overhanging with the gloomy hollows underneath. A watch was kept all night, and next day Captain Catling again dived repeatedly in an attempt to discover a trace of the vessel.[7]

On the third day a strong north-west wind came up, and the *Enterprise* had to head for the shelter of Carnley Harbour, where she remained weather-bound again for more than a month.

Catling then decided to go round the north of the islands, and anchor in North Harbour. From there they went down the west coast, and again tried to dive in the cove. But Catling 'had got only one dive in when the wind veered round, and the crew had to clear for their lives. The captain did not even have time to take off his diving dress. With his helmet off, he took the helm, while the crew got sail on the *Enterprise,* and she stood out of the cove and headed for Carnley Harbour.'

More bad weather followed, but eventually it cleared so that one day they were able to enter the cavern itself. As Captain Catling recalled,

> The sea on the western side was quite calm, and this time we were able to anchor the *Enterprise* right in the mouth of the cavern itself. I first examined the sea bottom just outside the cavern, especially alongside the buttress of rocks that stretched out into the southern

side of the cove and where it was reported in 1877 that the wreck of the *General Grant* could be seen, but all I found there was a ledge of rock – certainly not the length or breadth of a ship, but the ledge might have been mistaken for a sunken wreck, especially if the seekers were sounding with a fairly heavy sea running. We could see the loom of this rock from the surface of the water, the water being very clear indeed. If however, the water was a little bit thick, then no doubt anyone might mistake the ledge for a sunken rock. Anyway, there was no portion of the *General Grant* to be seen around there.[8]

And Catling had more than the dangers of the sea to contend with: he suddenly saw a seal heading towards him 'with the speed and force of a torpedo'.

I had, of course . . . my diver's knife, and with this I made a slice. However, when within a few feet of my helmet, the seal suddenly stopped, and then shot down beneath me, and came up for my legs. At this I kicked out, but missed him, and then I noticed that I was being carried towards an immense rock. As I looked the seal came over the top of the rock again, flying towards me, whereupon I thought I had better get up to the surface. Closing the valves in the helmet, I shot up like a rocket, surprising the crew, who could not understand what was happening. The next time I went down I took a bayonet, but I saw no more of the seal.[9]

This was the first expedition to actually put a diver down to explore the area.

In order to thoroughly examine the floor of the cove outside the cavern, Captain Catling was suspended in his diving dress beneath the vessel, which then steamed slowly over the locality. From this point of vantage he was enabled to see every detail of the bottom, and had any portion of the wreck or any gold bars been there he must have seen them – the floor being practically a level sheet of rock.

When a search of the cove did not reveal anything, Catling decided to go right into the cavern itself. When he discovered 'a number of pinnacle rocks at the bottom, on the outside of the cavern, . . . he came to the conclusion that it was absolutely impossible for any ship, once in the cavern, to slip back into deep water'. As he recalled:

We took a small anchor, and rowed into the cavern, and once there dropped the anchor, afterwards pulling the *Enterprise* stern first right inside also, until her mast was within a few feet of the roof and her stern so close that anyone leaning over the counter could have touched the rocks on one side – a very nice position had it come on to blow! The surge of the sea running into the cavern made diving so difficult that I was forced to use the rope leading to the anchor to pull myself into the cavern – a hard job with my diving suit on. Even with this aid I was badly knocked about amongst the boulders which strewed the bottom.[10]

The only indication he could find of a wreck was 'two pieces of timber jammed fast beneath some large boulders'. He was certain that 'the seas which come in with the north-west gales would in a short time smash any vessel into fragments'. Having closely examined the bottom of the cavern, he was satisfied that if the *General Grant*'s gold had been in the form of bars rather than dust, which was more likely, 'it must still have been there – that is, if it had not been recovered by somebody else. You must remember that gold is 12 times heavier than water. I can only come to one conclusion, and that is that the gold must have been recovered by some other expedition.' When asked by the reporter which expedition was most likely to have recovered the gold, Catling plumped for the *Daphne* in 1870: 'otherwise the disposal of such a large quantity of gold would certainly have leaked out in some way or other. The crew of the *Daphne*, however, were lost – and the treasure with them, if they really did secure it.'

It is interesting that Catling wrote of a cave so much like that described by the survivors, yet previous expeditions could not find it.

The cavern had a depth of 5 fathoms (30 ft.) at the mouth and three fathoms and a half towards the end. The main cavern was about 60 ft. high, running in from the mouth for a distance of about 200 yards. It was quite high enough to take a vessel in her whole length. The cavern narrowed towards the center, and then opened out into a large dome-shaped chamber at the end, which was higher and wider than the rest of the cave. At the end was a steep boulder beach. The *General Grant* could have got into the cavern quite easily, and after she had sunk, there would not have been much water over her. The cove outside the cavern had a depth of 11 fathoms close in and 15 fathoms further out.[11]

Catling returned to New Zealand discouraged and broke, having abandoned the *May Queen*, minus its engine, either in Port Ross or in Port Pegasus on Stewart Island. He was also facing prosecution by the Marine Department for sailing without a qualified crew as required by the Shipping and Seamen Act 1908. He had been notified of the regulations on 3 March (six days before the planned departure date) and prior to departure he had wired asking if the vessel could sail under the category of a pleasure yacht, but permission was denied. Determined to go, he had immediately set sail without the required crew.[12]

On their return, the *Evening Post* of 25 July 1916 reported that the Marine Department did not wish 'to press for a heavy penalty, as the defendant had lost heavily over the venture'. Catling explained that when he bought the *Enterprise* he was told that 'no certificated officers would be required'; and nothing had been said when he went to the Aucklands with two men in 1915. 'The vessel was really a pleasure yacht. She carried no passengers and no cargo, and no paid crew. They were simply on shares. He used the vessel for exploration purposes. He had lost all his money after many months of hardship.' Catling got off very lightly: the maximum penalty was £100 but he was fined £5, and costs of £2 9s. Catling had no further interest in the *General Grant*. 'It may be a land of fabulous gold treasure, but I have had enough trials and face to face talks with death in those latitudes to last me for the rest of my life.'[13]

Existing correspondence reveals that from the mid 1930s, the New Zealand Marine Department informed several prospective salvors of the *General Grant* that Captain Catling possessed notes made by a *General Grant* survivor (presumably James Teer). Perhaps unhelpfully, however, they do not seem to have provided an address where Captain Catling could be contacted.

Catling was not the only one to show interest while World War One raged on the other side of the world. In January 1916, C.E. Stratham, MP wrote to the Minister of Marine, Robert McNab, on behalf of his constituent William Davidson of Dunedin. The chairman of an unnamed company, Davidson requested the government's assurance 'that in the event of their being successful in recovering any of the gold or other valuables from the wreck the Crown will make no claim'. Stratham acknowledged that legislation would be necessary for this to occur but asked if it could be passed in the next parliamentary session. He pointed out that some lobbying had already occurred with several influential MPs who seemed to be in favour of the efforts and wishes of the Dunedin company, which had a vessel ready to sail to the Aucklands. Stratham argued that

> it would be in the interest of the Dominion that the company be given the desired permission to recover and retain the treasure, as it would mean so much added capital to the country. It is a venture that the Government itself would not be justified in undertaking, and it seems a pity to allow the gold to lie at the bottom of the sea if private people are willing to go to the expense and take the risk of trying to recover it. I feel that their enterprise and pluck deserve encouragement.[14]

A month later Stratham was advised that the Minister of Marine could 'give the Company a written assurance that in the event of the gold being recovered from this wreck and no claim being established by the former owners the Minister will allow the Company by way of salvage the full amount so recovered'. In spite of Stratham's sterling efforts on behalf of his constituent, there is no record of William Davidson and his syndicate mounting an expedition to the Aucklands.

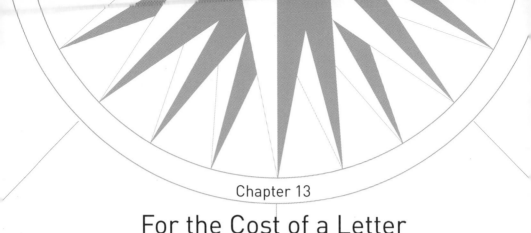

Chapter 13

For the Cost of a Letter

Once the war ended in 1918, enquiries about the *General Grant* began again in earnest.

Lewis A. Stockley of San Francisco got no further than writing to the Attorney General in February 1919. He was a member of a salvage company 'engaged principally in recovering vessels that have been sunk at sea'. He had records and information about the *General Grant* and believed that he and his colleagues had 'a method for the successful recovery of said vessel'. Despite their hopes, nothing more was heard from them.[1]

It was not until 18 October 1920 that the first enquiry came from a European country, when Alfred Gille Jorgensen from Denmark wrote to the Crown Solicitor, E.Y. Redwood. Jorgensen 'and a few others' had decided to search for the *General Grant*: they had 'a new Idea, besides some experience in diving and money to spend on it'. What they wanted was a permit to work on the wreck, but the government responded negatively and the Danes were not heard from again.

On 22 May 1923 the *New Zealand Times* picked up a small article that had appeared in the Melbourne *Argus*. Some time before, the *Argus* had reported that an Australian company, Marine Treasures Limited, had been formed to recover the *General Grant*'s gold and was proposing to leave in June or July of that year. A good deal of research appeared to have been undertaken and seemingly credible people were involved. Alfred Gale, a retired postmaster and mariner, and Wilfred Hughes, a surgeon from Melbourne, were already on the board; the other directors were still to be appointed. Of the 20,000 shares (£1 each) 10,000 were being offered for public subscription, 9000 shares were being allotted to the promoters and underwriters and the remaining 1000 would be divided among the divers. If the prospectus was to be believed anyone with capital to invest could earn a great return.[2]

The document contained a number of interesting statements, including the fact that 'most authentic sources furnished by the Australian and New Zealand governments' indicated that the nine tons of spelter and the 170 packages/sundries also constituted bullion. 'All data at hand prove conclusively that the cargo of this vessel is the richest of any known in the maritime world. Records, the conditions prevailing at the time of this wreck, and every evidence obtainable on both sides of the ocean go to corroborate the belief that this boat contains upwards of twenty millions of dollars' worth of gold and other cargo.'

The promoters would 'get to work on the *General Grant*, and, if successful, carry on salvage operations of other wrecks and treasure of which the promoters have particulars and location'. The company proposed to make what could almost be described as a tour of the Pacific. It would first salvage 'a cargo of between 200 and 300 tons of copper, valued at between £15,000 and £20,000 on an atoll in the Pacific'. Then it would head for northern Australia to recover a cargo whose value 'cannot be properly estimated, but certainly, if recovered, . . . will yield many thousands of pounds. The sole survivor of a party who knew the exact location of this cargo or "plant" will accompany the expedition.' The expedition would have a 'wireless outfit and operator, also a cinematographer, so that shareholders will be kept in close touch with what it is "doing" throughout. The film rights will be disposed of to the best advantage.'

Although the undertaking was 'more or less of the nature of a gamble', the directors assured readers of the prospectus that 'the men who have promoted and will control and carry out all these operations are of the highest integrity, experience, and ability, thoroughly understanding every branch of the work to be done'. With the appliances and methods which will be placed at their disposal, these men, fully prepared for the many hardships and life risks which confront them are unitedly determined to bring back with them to the State of Victoria, which it originally came from, the whole or part of this wonderful sunken treasure of the *General Grant* particularly, if it be humanly possible to do so, and also the other treasure referred to. Should either of the first two places mentioned be successfully exploited the Company should make very substantial profit; but if the *General Grant's* treasure be recovered the probabilities are that from it alone for every £1 invested each shareholder will receive more than a hundredfold.[3]

To add even more credence to their claims, they provided a note from a civil engineer – unnamed, like most people in this document – testifying to the fact that while in Invercargill, appearing before the Lands Board concerning the concession of the *General Grant*, he had been directed to a 'Mr. W.' in Bluff, who had seen the wreck while sealing at the Aucklands and 'could give me up-to-date information'. As was covered in Chapter 11, the prospectus quoted the mysterious 'Captain B', who claimed to have made expeditions to the Aucklands in 1887 and 1908. 'I hold myself – and no one else – the sole right to the land where the wreck is. No other party can use this. The Lands Office drew particular notice to this in their communications to me.' (A large question mark, initialled 'G.J.' of the Marine Department, appears beside the engineer's statement about 'Mr W.' in the copy of the prospectus held in Archives New Zealand.)[4]

It all sounded irresistible, but there were concerns about the company's claim. The Director of Navigation in Melbourne forwarded a copy of the prospectus to the Chief Surveyor of the New Zealand Lands and Survey Department, noting that Gale and Hughes claimed to have been 'nominated by the holders of the New Zealand Government's Salvage Rights to the *General Grant*'. A prompt explained that the lease in force had been granted in September 1920 to William Johnson Spence (who may possibly have been connected to the James Spence whom James Teer knew) and that the rent of £2 per annum was paid up to 19 September 1923. So was Captain B an out-and-out liar, or did he hold the secret in pursuit of which so much effort, money and lives had been squandered to date? He certainly gave seemingly plausible excuses why no gold had been recovered on either of his purported expeditions: 'I have come to the conclusion that the only way to conduct successful salvage operations is to work from the top of the rocks immediately over where the wreck lies. If this were done the work of salving will be easy, as there will be power enough and to spare to lift the rocks off her decks, which would be preferable to the use of dynamite, and so get access to her hold.'

The prospectus also quoted statements by Catling which directly repeat what he had told the press – though, of course, it could be argued that Catling too was playing his cards very close to his chest.

With reference to the question as to the action of the sea-worm upon the timbers of wrecked vessels, Captain Catling has proved conclusively that the damage done is inconsiderable. In order to satisfy himself he visited the site of the wreck of the *Grafton* in Carnley Harbour, Auckland Island, and his special apparatus for observation under water disclosed the timbers of the frame of the *Grafton* quite unaffected. The *Grafton* was wrecked in 1864, two years earlier than the *General Grant*, and furthermore, the *Grafton* is in the milder waters of a harbour, while the *General Grant* lies on the exposed west coast, where the action of the worm would be still less. Under these circumstances, Captain Catling is satisfied that the gold in the *General Grant* will still be in its boxes and that the frame of the vessel will be perfectly sound.

Only two other items remain in the file – an application form sent to the New Zealand government so that any interested party could buy shares, and a plaintive letter from a gentleman in Southland, written in 1926.

> Perhaps you might let me know if the *General Grant* has been salvaged. I understand the Company MTL applied to the New Zealand Government to right of salvage. I took out some shares in the company and the last advise [*sic*] I received was about the beginning of 1925 it said they were going down shortly to start operations. I wrote 9 months ago and had my letter returned. I wrote a second time but so far have had no reply so I am writing this thinking you might know something . . .[5]

The Minister of Marine wrote a brief note, which must have been disheartening, if not devastating, to the investor. 'So far as this department is aware none of the endeavours which have been made to salvage the gold alleged to be in the wreck have been successful. So far as the company known as MTL is concerned I understand this company holds or did hold the rights to the shore in the locality, but so far as the right to salvage the hulk or any other cargo are concerned, no application for permission to do so has been received by this department.'[6]

The fame of the *General Grant* and her treasure was spreading, and more letters were coming in from all over the world. By now the New Zealand Marine Department had developed a form letter to reply to these would-be treasure seekers. One of these was sent to Svend Steffensen from Copenhagen, who wrote to the Maritime Court in Wellington in

October 1924 asking a number of very basic questions about the amount of gold the ship was carrying when she went down, the exact spot where she went down, how much it would cost to obtain permission to work the wreck and finally where to obtain such permission – in fact 'all the papers concerning this matter...'[7]

The next year, having made 'several unsuccessful attempts . . .to work the wreck', Steffensen wrote to the Marine Department:

> We take the liberty of presuming that the Government has reserved the deal for other purposes. However, we claim that our five years work in this case has been so successful that we are able to offer you very favorable conditions, if possible we can obtain the enterprise for the Government.

He went on to explain that the Danes could make a successful salvage expedition for no more than £3,500. Their government would credit them with £500 'payable at any bank in Denmark, you should prefer, when the deal is properly closed by for instance the English Consul. The rest £3000 – is payable on our arrival in Wellington.' The salvors would claim 20 per cent of everything recovered from the wreck, excluding the expenses of the salvage. Not surprisingly, G.C. Godfrey, the Secretary of Marine, replied: 'I can not recommend that Mr. Steffensen's proposal be entertained'. [8]

Undeterred, Steffensen wrote once more in September 1926. He requested permission and asked for the rules of salvage, telling the New Zealand government that there would be only three members in the year-long expedition. He received a very curt note saying that the 1925 decision had not changed and that no permission would be granted.

It is intriguing that most of the subsequent enquiries made about the *General Grant* wreck came from New Zealand (in whose waters the ship sank), Australia (the ship left from Melbourne), the United States of America (she was an American vessel) and Scandinavia. There were no applications or enquiries from Britain or other parts of Western Europe at this time – except for Ireland, as both Teer and Caughey came from there.

Two budding entrepreneurs from Melbourne, Stephen C. Gillard and William Leslie, who obviously believed in going straight to the top, wrote to the New Zealand Prime Minister, Gordon Coates, whom they addressed as 'My Lord', on 28 October 1925. It is to be hoped that their treasure hunting skills were better than their letter writing.

You will pardon us for taking such a liberty of writing this letter. We wishes to inform you re the sinking ship that sank about Three King Islands some years ago of what we have been informed that she had a large amount of gold, we wishes to know of what would the government offer us if we should bring the gold to the surface. We have a device that we can guarantee to re-float any sunken ships. We were also informed that the drawback was to the divers was the octopus we can counteract all those difficulties. We were also informed that a ship is wedged in a cave and the difficulties was about getting to her is that the sea is always rough and she also has a large amount of gold in her. We have no difficulties of counteract the rough sea, in that respect we can guarantee you that this is a easy matter to be overcome, we would be very much obliged to you if you would entrain this matter and give it your immediate attention as we want to get to work while the summer season last.

As a bureaucrat's note in the margin pointed out, Gillard and Leslie were clearly confused: it was the *Elingamite* that had gone down at the Three Kings in 1902. They too received a 'no' letter.[9]

Another hopeful from Australia, named Harrison, wrote to the Under-Secretary for Internal Affairs, James Hislop, for details at the end of January 1928. He was forming a company to salvage the *General Grant* and he too planned to work from the cliffs above the wreck. He also received the brush-off letter with this added note: 'In regard to intention to work from cliffs over wreck, I have to inform you that Marine Treasures Ltd. hold, or did hold, the rights to the shore in the locality of the wreck and in a prospectus issued in 1923 alleged that it is from the land only that the treasure may be recovered'.[10]

Harrison wrote back on 9 February to point out that since Marine Treasures had failed to raise the capital required for the venture and had done nothing since 1923, he would like to purchase their lease. On 7 March he was informed that the Marine Treasures lease was due to expire on 15 September 1929. No more was heard from Harrison.

In 1930, J.H. Crawford of Oriental Bay in Wellington wrote to the Marine Department asking the by now familiar questions and adding that he wanted to take over the Marine Treasures concession when it expired. There appears to be considerable confusion regarding the ownership of the lease. Despite having told Harrison that the lease ran till September 1929, Godfrey wrote to Crawford on 28 January 1931 saying that Spence's 1920 yearly licence was still in force and the Lands

Department was unlikely to consider any other applications until it expired.

The confusion resulted partially from the fact that permission to land on the Auckland Islands and occupy areas of foreshore on the Islands, and particularly those adjacent to the supposed wreck site, was required from the Department of Lands and Survey, whereas those wishing to undertake salvage or to work on the wreck site had to seek the permission from the New Zealand Marine Department.

On 5 November 1931, Forman & Co. of Melbourne wrote with the same enquiry and received essentially the same answer. Forman then wrote back offering £10 a year as nominal holding rental. On 18 February 1932, the Department of Lands and Survey told the Secretary of the Marine that Spence's licence rent was £2 8s 10d in arrears. They had received a cheque towards it on 1 October 1931, but it had bounced. The last communication had been in January 1932.

On 27 April a Sydney real estate company asked about the rights of salvage and how to purchase them. Forman's suggestion of a £10 holding rental led the government to realise that the *General Grant* wreck could provide some income for their coffers simply by leasing the rights, and that £2 per annum was only a token. The Assistant Secretary of Marine suggested this to Lands and Survey, who promptly replied that the licence to Spence should be formally cancelled if payment was not received in the very near future. Then the licence could be granted to Forman, but the £10 should be for lease of the foreshore only, not the salvage rights. To clarify their position, W. Robinson of the Department of Lands and Survey told the Assistant Secretary of Marine in Wellington that his department was concerned only with the lease of the foreshore and 'if a syndicate is prepared to pay the rent suggested it does not appear to be the department's function to restrict private enterprise unduly'.

B.W. Miller of Lands and Survey was not impressed:

> The fact that your department is prepared to accept, and a syndicate is prepared to pay a rent in view of past experience in the matter of *General Grant* salvage and that your department is concerned only with the leasing of the access, while this department's interests are in the salvage this department is only foregoing 'the shadow' in endeavouring to enable your dept to obtain 'the substance'.[11]

On 27 April 1932, Australian Eugene J. Sheehy wrote to the New Zealand Marine Department, enquiring as to who held the rights to the *General Grant.* By April 1933 the Commissioner of Crown Lands had cancelled Spence's foreshore rights, and Sheehy was advised that the lease was available but that any expedition he mounted would not to be permitted to engage in sealing or to destroy any native birds on the islands. On 10 April 1933, the lease was granted to Sheehy.

Author Michael Hervey regards Eugene Sheehy as 'probably the unluckiest man of all' in respect of *General Grant* expeditions. Overall he wrote more than 1000 letters in his search for the legal owners of the *General Grant.* During 1937 and 1938 he turned down approaches from experienced Italian and Californian salvagers, believing that 'only good Australian men' should bring up the gold. In 1947, it was reported that another Australian syndicate, which included the well-known diver J.E. (Johnno) Johnstone (who had worked on the salvages of the *Niagara* and the *Wanganella* and was a good friend of Sheehy and his brother William, a Royal Australian Navy diver), had gone into partnership with Eugene Sheehy, V. H. Neilly and three others to recover the £3 million worth of gold from the *General Grant.* But nothing seems to have come of this venture. Sheehy dreamed that when retired he would have enough money to mount an expedition, but by the time he finished work in 1952 his health had failed.

On 4 December 1933, Captain H.E. Humphreys of Te Rou, Blenheim wrote requesting a permit and explaining that he had some valuable information for the Minister of the Marine: 'It may interest you to know that the ship can be boarded at low tide, the decks then being only covered with three or four feet of water, that she is fully protected from further storm damage.' In a second letter in January 1934, which he wanted kept confidential, Humphreys suggested sending the government steamer *Matai* to recover the 'six million pounds worth of gold'. He also claimed to have in his syndicate a man who went on an expedition to the Auckland Islands thirty years earlier when the ship's cook had found the wreck while out hunting goats.[12]

During 1934 and 1935 there was a flurry of overseas interest in the *General Grant* wreck. In September 1934, for example, G.M. Duncan of Melbourne wrote to the New Zealand Marine Department, requesting a licence to salvage the *General Grant.* Then in December 1934, Gilbert Parmelec of Seattle, Washington wrote seeking information about the *'President Grant'* [*sic*]. That month also brought a letter from John

R. Sanders of Calgary, Canada, claiming that a relative of his, one H. Newman, was a miner returning to England on the *General Grant* and that he had given his gold to the captain, who had stored it in his cabin. He was told that the Marine Department had no records of who was lost in the wreck. The name Charles Newman (an English miner) does in fact appear on the passenger list (see Appendix II).

When G.L. Gaskell wrote from Alhambra, California in January 1935, stating that their syndicate, which included both American and Canadian interests, had new 'Deep Sea Diving Equipment' that could be used in up to 170 fathoms, they were told that Eugene Sheehy of Sydney held the rights and that Captain Percy Catling possessed the notes made by one of the *General Grant* survivors (presumably James Teer). Robert Bruce of South Melbourne also wrote in 1935 asking if permission was needed to search for and work on the wreck. He too was informed that Sheehy held the rights. The final major enquiry of 1935, in November, came from the Romano Marine Salvage Syndicate of Seattle, which was planning a salvage attempt using the 'Romano Sphere', a type of diving bell, on board their vessel the *Constellation*. They were given the by now familiar information about Sheehy and Catling.

There was New Zealand interest too. An item in the *Dominion* of 26 February 1935 stated that a young Auckland engineer, D.P.L. Twiss, was to leave for the Auckland Islands in one to two months. He would purchase or charter a schooner and had been collecting information about the wreck and subsequent expeditions. He proposed to take a crew of 12 and to stay down there for nine months. Twiss had designed a special diving helmet that was larger than normal as it contained an electronic depth gauge and a telephone for communication. In addition to the schooner, he proposed to take a heavy-duty launch and a 3½-kilowatt radio transmitter 'for telephonic messages'.

Twiss believed that the spelter listed on the manifest was in fact gold. He had made 'exhaustive geological researches' and claimed that he was certain of the 'location of the crevasse'. He also believed that previous expeditions had searched in the wrong location and that their equipment was inadequate for the great depths found at the Aucklands.

A later report in the *New Zealand Truth* on 4 September 1935 stated that Twiss was going to acquire the schooner *Aratapu* and that he had exchanged letters with Sheehy: they were going to work together on an expedition. On 9 March 1935 *Truth* reported that Twiss and Sheehy believed that the nine tons of spelter was in fact gold and that on the strength of that a £50,000 company was to be floated in Sydney. By

14 September 1935 the *Dominion* was reporting that 21-year-old Auckland engineer Dennis Penn Lascelles, 'who was to lead the *General Grant* expedition' – presumably the Twiss/Sheehy expedition – to recover £2,500,000 worth of gold, had been jailed for six months for stealing car parts. It is tempting to speculate on the identity of Twiss and Lascelles. Is it a coincidence that both men were engineers in Auckland, both had the same first initials D.P., and both (according to press reports) were about to lead expeditions to hunt for the gold on the *General Grant*? Lascelles had previously been had up for stealing car parts. Did he change his name to Twiss in order to start over, only to revert to his old ways and wind up in prison?

From the end of 1935 to the outbreak of the Second World War the Marine Department received only two minor enquiries about the *General Grant*. One, in 1937, was from a J.W.R. Sanders in Vancouver who wanted a list of passengers, details of previous salvage attempts and the address of Captain Catling. The Marine Department replied that they had no idea where Catling was. The other, in 1939, came from H. Lewis of Takaka near Nelson, who enquired whether the gold belonged to the New Zealand government and whether he could gain the rights to recover it.

As had been the case between 1914 and 1918, there were no salvage queries during the Second World War. The populace was focused on the conflict and there was a shortage of divers, suitable vessels and capital to invest in treasure hunting.

The first post-war enquiry did not arrive until 1949, when one N. Christensen of Denmark asked about the gold lost in Sarah's Bosom and wanted the rights to salvage treasure worth several million Danish crowns. He was informed that any gold recovered must be declared to the New Zealand Receiver of Wrecks, that some believed that the spelter on board the *General Grant* was 46 per cent gold but that there was 'no verification of this statement' and Sheehy still held the licence.

It is now that Harry Marfleet (already mentioned as the author of a play about the *General Grant*) re-enters the story. In the *Grimsby Evening Telegraph* of 11 March 1949, Marfleet was reported as saying: 'Now we are concentrating on an old sailing ship wreck which is supposed to have £3,000,000 in gold bars in her cargo.'

A former Cleethorpes man who emigrated to Australia with his wife and two step-sons 24 years ago, is to attempt to salvage £3,000,000 in gold bars from the depths of the Pacific Ocean next summer. She lies 90 feet beneath the waves, in a cavern 285 miles south of South Island, New Zealand.

Mr. Harry Marfleet tells the story in his own words:

'I was mixed up with Diver John Johnson [*sic*], the man who got £2,300,000 out of the wreck of the *Niagara* in 1941-42. He left £151,000 in gold bars because, as they were in the far corner of the strong room, he could not reach them. It would have been possible to reach them with an extending grab attachment fixed on his diving bell and operated from within. However, it is all washed up for the time being because the costs have beat us.

'Now we are concentrating on an old sailing ship wreck which is supposed to have £3,000,000 in gold bars in her cargo. She is the U.S.A. sailing ship, *General Grant*, wrecked when bound from Melbourne to London in May 1881 [sic].

'Three syndicates have tried to get her opened up but have failed because of the treacherous weather. It is on Auckland Island, 285 miles south of the main south island of New Zealand.

'I and two old retired friends now propose to equip an expedition next summer have a try to get a diver down to her. We think at this early stage that if we blast the cavern cliff down in front of the wreck, it will keep the heavy seas out and our diver will then be able to work in calm waters.

'We do not think we will be called upon to put down too much money as a Press agency and film company will pay us big money to go along for a story and pictures.'

Harry Marfleet's father, Mr. Samuel Marfleet, who last month celebrated his 90th birthday, told an *Evening Telegraph* reporter today, 'Harry always was an adventurer. I suppose it was the "wanderlust" in him that made him give up a flourishing business and emigrate to Australia. One day, business was as usual. Two days later he had tied it up and had made all arrangements to emigrate. He was like that.'

On 13 June 1950, the *Auckland Star* reported that a Sydney business-man, Harry Marfleet, who was among the salvage crew working on the wreck of the *Marietta Dal* off Moreton Island in Australia, hoped to recover £500,000 worth of gold from the *General Grant*. Marfleet apparently had in his possession notes written by William Sanguilly, who was the 'last man to leave the wreck and was in charge of the cargo. Under the Captain's instructions Mr Sanguilly had a special consignment marked as spelter, copper ore [*sic*] to deceive certain ex-convicts and possible pirates among the crew and passengers.' (As mentioned earlier, in Marfleet's play Sanguilly was put in charge of loading the gold on board the *General Grant*.)

Marfleet deposited the outline of his play with the Commonwealth of Australia Copyright Office, but no more was heard of his proposed expedition and his rather grandiose scheme of blasting the cliffs in front of the cavern so that their diver could work in relatively calm seas.

Two interesting enquiries were received in 1952 from Newcastle, County Down, Northern Ireland, the home town of James Teer and Patrick Caughey, both survivors of the *General Grant*. One came from Daniel Teer, a great-nephew of James Teer, who had seen a reference to the planned Johnstone/Sheehy expedition and wanted to make a claim to a portion of the gold on behalf of his two sisters and himself. He was informed that any gold recovered belonged to the Crown and any claimants would have to prove that any found belonged to James Teer. The second letter was sent by Thomas Fegan, who claimed that he was related to Caughey and registered his interest should any gold be found.[13]

The *New Zealand Herald* of 23 June 1954 reported that Auckland scrap-metal dealer Charles Levard was leading a team of Aucklanders to salvage the wreck of the *General Grant*. 'There is a fortune waiting for anyone wanting to pick it up,' he said. By late August Levard had reached an agreement with the New Zealand government about sharing the proceeds of the *General Grant* salvage; he was planning to leave Auckland in the fishing trawler *Waipu*. Initially he had bought the former Waiheke Island ferry *Tangaroa* but found that it would cost too much money to convert it for treasure hunting. With a crew of three he intended to arrive at the Auckland Islands in mid-October 1954.[14]

Levard's was not the only expedition planned at this time. By the mid-1950s two other groups were preparing to search for the *General Grant*: a Dunedin expedition and an attempt led by Australian Bill Havens.

It was reported in the *Dunedin Star* in July 1954 that a group of young Dunedin men were going after the 500,000 pounds worth of treasure on the *General Grant*. It was hoped that a diver with experience at

Zeebrugge and Normandy (with a knowledge of underwater explosives) would join them and they were making enquiries in Dunedin and Bluff for a suitable charter vessel to tackle 'the job' in the winter of 1955.

The *Otago Daily Times* of 14 September 1954 reported that the Dunedin syndicate (which included a medical student) were convinced that the gold was still there and that they had been in touch with Mr M.J.Olsen, a 71-year-old Swede, who had taken part in the 1916 Catling expedition. It is likely that these two reports in July and September 1954 were about the same proposed expedition.

The third proposed expedition was to be led by Australian mining engineer William Joseph (Bill) Havens. Bill Havens is one of the most colourful characters in the *General Grant* story. He was born in 1919 and, as the *Scottish Sunday Express* of 4 August 1954 reported, he 'left home to cut sugar cane when he was 19, chased saboteurs with the American Navy, mined in Mexico, South Africa and America. Then he heard of the gold.' The *Junior Mirror* of 24 November 1954 described him as a former private detective, lumberjack, big-game hunter and mining engineer.

He managed to amass enough capital to buy a salvage vessel and mount an expedition to find the *General Grant*. He purchased the rights to the wreck from Eugene Sheehy and early in 1954, with about $US20,000, he travelled to Scotland, bought an old fishing vessel from a scrapyard on the Clyde and began equipping her. He selected a crew from hundreds of applications, ending up with a selection that sounds like the beginning of a joke. There was Bill the Australian skipper, Welshman Gus Sullivan, Scotsman John 'Ginger' Ritchie (carpenter) and Cornishman Glyn Davys (engineer). On the voyage down to London, the vessel's engine broke down and she drifted in the North Sea before being towed into the English port of Boston so the damage could be repaired.

During their time in Boston a writ was nailed to the mast of the vessel relating to an incident in the Firth of Forth when the vessel was helped off a mudbank by an Admiralty tug. In addition, they were desperately short of money and Havens told the *Scottish Sunday Express*: 'My crew don't live on birdseed.' Sullivan was also quoted in the article as saying: 'Oh, we are managing to survive. We are hoping to get some night work on the dock to help us out a bit. We can't work during the day – we spend that working on the boat.'

When Levard, from the Auckland-based expedition, heard of his rival's misfortune, he said, 'Good luck, Mr Havens'.[15]

Havens finally set out for New Zealand in 1955 from the Channel Islands on the 65-foot motor vessel *Absit Omen* (the name means 'let no evil befall').[16] Technology had advanced greatly since the Second World War: the expedition carried the very latest diving equipment and an underwater television camera to be used for the first exploratory work. This camera had earlier been used in salvaging the wreckage of a crashed Comet aircraft off the island of Elba. Initially on board were skipper 35-year-old Havens, mate John 'Ginger' Ritchie, aged 26, a shipwright from Govan, Glasgow; John Clements, aged 22, from Bulawayo, Southern Rhodesia, chief engineer; 21-year-old John Peter Holliday from Durban (a former Air Force pilot), 29-year-old Peter Nye from Perth, Western Australia, navigator; 23-year-old Harry Green, cook, and his 21-year-old brother Vernon Green, who were both also from Perth. David Bowman, a young Australian journalist, also joined the crew. The final name on the muster roll was Boston, the ship's cat.

According to an article in the *Sunday Telegraph* of 17 March 1957, three of the Australians in the crew (Nye and the Green brothers) had fallen out with Havens and left the expedition before the *Absit Omen* cleared English waters. The same article reported that the vessel tied up in Tangier on Christmas Eve 1954 and the crew were flat broke. Two German hands – Paul Mollem, aged 45, and Ulrich Lucks, aged 27, described as being of 'doubtful backgrounds' – wanted to get to Australia and each paid more than one hundred pounds passage money. That got the vessel as far as Port Said. David Bowman reported that 'by then we were living on boiled onions and rough flour cakes fried in suntan lotion. Havens was broke again.'

They made it through the Suez Canal and out into the Red Sea bound for Port Sudan. But their voyage came to a dramatic end when *Absit Omen* struck a mischarted reef in the Red Sea near Port Sudan, on the African coast halfway between Suez and Aden. David Bowman described what happened:

We crashed onto Elba Reef, 150 miles north of Port Sudan at 4:30 on Tuesday morning. As we heeled over in the darkness rollers crashed down the companionway, flooding the accommodation.

The vessel was listing at 45 degrees and a bell was tolling mournfully as each sea struck. The radio went dead, and we could not launch the boat because of the list, for more than an hour. Five men manned the boat, and we set out, towing two in the rubber dinghy.

We battled for 10 backbreaking hours against winds and currents before landing exhausted at nightfall, 12 miles away.[17]

Once ashore, they were rescued by a Sudanese cowherd who sent his brother on a 40-mile camel trip for help across the desert and brought back a rescue party after what Bowman termed 'three days of hardships and living with natives at a desert outpost'. When found, the seven men were 'unkempt, unshaven, sunburnt and ragged'.

When they returned to the *Absit Omen* for their gear, they found that the vessel had been stripped by Arab pirates. Havens returned to Australia, via Sri Lanka, on a liner: he was classified as a 'destitute seaman'. Once back in Sydney, he sold his car and as a result of publicity was able to borrow several thousand pounds. He then worked his passage to England in order to purchase another vessel. At Inverkeithing on the Firth of Forth he found a 78-ton ex-Admiralty salvage yacht which was sold to him as scrap.

Using his remaining funds, he refurbished the vessel and purchased underwater equipment including an underwater television camera. Havens had intended to name the vessel *Absit Omen II* but decided that *Goldseeker* was a better bet'.[18]

In a letter to the New Zealand Commissioner of Crown Lands in February 1956, Havens claimed that two of the 'interested parties' in the expedition were Captain Daniel McLaughlan and Martin Pool (McLaughlan was second mate of the *Dundonald* and Martin – elsewhere named Michael – Pul was either a Russian or Finnish ordinary seaman). Both were survivors of the wreck of the *Dundonald* on the Auckland Islands in 1907. Then in the spring of 1956, with fellow Australian Ron Smith, Cardiff-born Gus O'Sullivan and four other unnamed crew, Havens set out on the 14,000-mile voyage to the Auckland Islands. The journey was dogged by a series of engine breakdowns, gales and accidents. Then, off the coast of Timor, *Goldseeker* struck a reef and had to be abandoned. Havens braved mountains and thick jungle to get help.

Meanwhile the other six men set out in a lifeboat for Australia and were rescued close to death on Bathurst Island two weeks later.[19]

Bob Addison, a former Tauranga (New Zealand) city councillor, wrote an interesting account of his voyage on the *Goldseeker* which was published in *Waterline* magazine during 2006-07. Bob and his brother Alan, both in their early twenties, were travelling overland from Europe back to their native New Zealand, where Alan was due to be married. Having arrived in Singapore, they looked for a vessel to take them home, heard about *Goldseeker* and were offered a passage for a sum of money which they agreed to pay when they reached Australia.

The crew of *Goldseeker* had undergone a number of changes since leaving Europe. On the muster roll as the vessel left Singapore were: Bill Havens, skipper; Verity Gill (23), an Indian journalist from Singapore (who was designated as cook, even though he couldn't!); Arthur Danaher (42), an Irishman who was the engineer and had been with Havens the longest; Chang San Yapp (31) from Singapore, also known as 'Tapps'; and a mysterious North American known as 'Buddy', who had plenty of money to pay his passage. He later gave his name to the Australian authorities (and to reporters) as James Burke (34), a seaman from Vancouver, British Columbia, but his real name was Darwin Beers. He had escaped from a chain-gang while serving a ten-year jail sentence in Florida for armed robbery. He then made his way to Japan where he was recaptured by the FBI but managed to get away from them in Singapore and joined *Goldseeker*. Three of the crew – Gill, Danaher and Burke/Beers – lacked passports and hoped they could slip into Australia unnoticed by the authorities.

From Singapore, *Goldseeker* headed down to Bali in Indonesia, but because of internal political turmoil they were not allowed to land. They were kept under armed guard while two crew members were allowed to go ashore to buy provisions. When they left they were forbidden to land at any other Indonesian port.

Their next port of call was Dili in Portuguese Timor where the local authorities (unlike the Indonesians) were very helpful, but after three days' stay, they set sail again. Havens announced that he would like to go hunting, so *Goldseeker* sailed to a beautiful little lagoon called Lornie on the south coast of Timor and anchored. Addison claims that although at the time Havens' decision to go hunting came across as a spontaneous decision, 'subsequent events indicated that this was part of a carefully worked out insurance scam'.

While Havens was hunting, a tropical storm suddenly blew up and *Goldseeker* ran aground. The remaining crew considered trying to winch the vessel off but there were no suitable rocks or trees on which to anchor the winch, so they decided to wait for high tide. At the right time, with Havens at the controls, Addison reported that Bill put the ship into full ahead (which he claimed was an accident), and the vessel went further aground and stuck fast. Havens borrowed a horse and set out for Dili, with a guide, in order to contact his insurance company about the salvage of *Goldseeker* and to send back assistance and more stores. He said that he had made arrangements with the natives to feed the crew until his return. That was the last the crew ever saw of Bill Havens.

Havens' family disputes that the wrecking of the *Goldseeker* was an insurance scam, and in an email to the author in January 2008, his son Tony Havens states: 'He [Bill] had spent many years and a lot of capital and effort to get to this point, I doubt if the measly insurance compensation from one old wooden boat would have compensated him for his efforts – especially as he was so close this time. If he had wanted to wreck the boat, the English Channel would have done just as well. Why sail another 10,000 miles in great hardship?'

The crew waited, and although the locals were friendly, they insisted on payment for the food with items of clothing. Two Portuguese officials arrived and ordered the crew not to leave the village or the vessel, stating that Havens would soon return. Sick of the monotonous diet, mindful of their dwindling stock of surplus clothing and believing that the insurance cover on the *Goldseeker* would probably not cover the cost of salvage in so remote a location, they decided on self-rescue.

The six men set out across the 400-mile Timor Sea bound for Australia in the ship's 16-foot lifeboat, with a mast cut from the Timor bush and improvised sails. All they had for navigation was a small plastic compass and a Collins *School Atlas*. The only food they had was a pig, 30 coconuts and some bunches of bananas.

Initially they sailed south, but a fearful storm on the second night broke their mast and they had to take turns all night to support it. When an aeroplane flew overhead, making for what they believed was Darwin, Burke/Beers took a bearing on the plane and they altered their course to south-west. He was the only crew member with any seafaring experience, having served on a sailing ship between Cuba and Florida. Addison credits him with saving their lives.

They eventually sighted a lighthouse on what turned out to be Bathurst Island, but their lifeboat was wrecked on landing and they spent three days wandering around looking for food. Fortunately they were found by two miners who lived on the island, and the Royal Australian Navy tug *Emu* rescued them and transported them to Darwin where they were immediately taken to hospital. A report in the *Dominion* of 13 March 1957 states: 'They had been at sea for eighteen days and had covered more than 300 miles in their motorless dinghy. All were bearded, thin, badly sunburnt and clad only in tattered clothing.' By then, three of them were stretcher cases but they all soon recovered. Burke/Beers had given a name and address to the media, and the story was picked up by the Canadian media, who checked out his Canadian address which proved to be false. The FBI were informed and Burke/Beers was arrested when he was discharged from hospital.

Havens reached Singapore as a crew member on a Dutch cargo ship from Timor, where he told newsmen he was going to claim the insurance on *Goldseeker* and return to England to buy a third vessel. But at this point the intrepid Bill Havens disappears from the *General Grant* story. However, he continued with his adventurous life, driving overland from Singapore to England in a Land Rover in 1957 and fathering seven known children to several different women. He died in Norway in 1977 while on a voyage delivering a vessel from Tromso to the Mediterranean. He is buried at Grantchester, near Cambridge in England.

Nothing more was heard of the plans of the other two proposed expeditions from the mid 1950s either. Charles Levard and his fishing trawler *Waipu* and the Dunedin syndicate who had consulted M. J. Olsen about the *General Grant* joined the ever-growing ranks of dreamers in the saga.

On 11 March 1949, the *Grimsby Evening Telegraph* (which had earlier carried the story of Harry Marfleet's expedition plans) also published a rather bizarre story about a syndicate represented by Neil Shirtliffe, a mechanic for a Wellington earth-moving firm, who, with a team of five other New Zealanders, had applied to the Department of Lands and Survey for a permit in 1969. Shirtliffe admitted that neither he nor his companions had 'any ability or background of skin-diving'. They proposed to charter a ship and helicopter and create a road across the island with bulldozers to a point above the wreck site. Harking back to the *Flora* expedition of 1876, their plan was to blast material from the top of the cliff, thus creating a dam in front of the cave. They would then pump the water out and be free to mine the area within. His plan was demolished when the application was denied because of the damage that would be done to the area. The syndicate appealed, and on 10 September 1969 the Outlying Islands Committee agreed to recommend a permit to land on the main Auckland Island with the proviso that bulldozers and explosives not be used. Not surprisingly, nothing more was heard from Shirtliffe and his team.[20]

In 1971 the Secretary of Marine wrote to unidentified 'Canadian interests' discouraging them from even considering mounting an expedition. He pointed out that apart from the danger, and the number of previous unsuccessful attempts, '… our records show the possibility of at least 5 claims from descendants of persons on the boat at the time of the wreck and in the event of any gold being found any representations from these claimants would need to be taken into account.'

This seems to have deterred the 'Canadian interests' but certainly not the New Zealanders.

Chapter 14

Modern Days

It is perhaps surprising, considering the tremendous developments in diving technology and underwater recovery over the last 30 to 40 years, that there have been no breakthroughs in the finding of the wreck of the *General Grant*. Hard hats and hubble bubbles (a later variation on the hard hat, with air pumped from the surface but without the full diving suit and suitable only for relatively shallow water) have given way to scuba gear; laborious manhandling of debris to high-pressure hoses, venturis (powerful vacuum cleaners that can move small rocks and other material away from a wreck), lift bags and heavy-duty lifting gear; and spotting of hopeful shapes has given way to magnetometers. But still the wreck of the *General Grant* has not been found.

By 1970 Kelly Tarlton from the Bay of Islands, New Zealand was becoming a legend in his own time as an underwater photographer, adventurer and treasure hunter. His first success was almost accidental when, on a general diving trip to the Three Kings Islands in 1965, his group found the *Elingamite*. From this wreck they recovered $12,000 in gold and silver coins. It would be only natural that at some point he would tackle the *General Grant*. The first of the 'modern' expeditions was that of the Historical Wreck syndicate formed by Tarlton, Bill and John Gallagher and John Pettit. It left New Zealand on 23 January 1970 on board the 88-foot motorised yacht *Hamutana*, based in Tauranga.

Leaving Bluff, as so many previous *General Grant* expeditions had done, they followed the time-honoured practice of holing up at Stewart Island while they waited for the weather to clear. They drank with the local fishermen and dived on various local wrecks. According to John Dearling, one of the five divers on the expedition, it was just as well they were all good mates, because 'breakfast was *always* bacon, eggs, weetbix and peaches, and dinner was *always* roast beef and vegetables, topped with more peaches.'

On arriving at the Auckland Islands they found the 'Cave of Death' quite easily. Kelly Tarlton is quoted as saying, 'That's the one.' He had done a considerable amount of research on the wreck of the *General Grant* and even had a photograph of the cave.

John Dearling later described what happened:

> Our hearts were beating with excitement and steam came off our breath as the master plan was made. Kelly and I were to dive first, swim into the cave, mark the gold position and then everyone would help raise it. (Just like that – no worries.) We jumped into the water and our warm bodies were soon shaking. Five minutes and our fingers were hopeless. The current swept in and we would move in with it at about 15 m.p.h. then hang on whilst it raced out again.

Nothing was initially found until Don Lock (a cook and boatman on the expedition) found an anchor which, although cemented to a rock, was soon removed using half a plug of gelignite and brought on board. It later proved to be an anchor lost by Percy Catling on the 1915-16 expedition. The divers saw albatross bones and 'bones that looked human but could have been from seals', but no gold – not even any ships. 'It was a bitter blow to everyone that nothing was to be found.'[1]

The expedition spent about a week at the Auckland Islands. Between dives they spent time on the islands, visiting the castaway depots and the remains of the wreck of the *Grafton*. They also went hunting and fishing to supplement their rather limited diet. Having done 80 dives and checked some 50 caves further down the coast, they returned empty-handed. The trip back to Tauranga was uneventful (except for some very rough seas) with stops being made on the Southland coast for more wreck-diving and some fishing.[2]

It was reported in the press in November 1971 that the motor vessel *Picton* had been chartered by a group of Wellington men and fitted out for an expedition to search for the *General Grant's* gold. Built in 1917 as a steamer, the *Picton* was later converted to a motor ship. At the time of the charter she was a fishing boat at the Chatham Islands under the command of the well-known Wellington master, Captain Alan Aberdeen.

The *Auckland Star*'s shipping reporter (and maritime historian) Allan A. Kirk, commented that if they did return with booty, it would be 'one of the miracles of this century'.³

It would seem that the press got it wrong. The *Picton* was in fact chartered by Victoria University and the crew included geology professor John Bradley and his Canadian colleague Bill Knox. They did indeed go to the Auckland Islands and to Campbell Island in the hope of finding valuable tin deposits, not gold. They did not even have diving gear with them, though they set a few pots in the hope of catching spider crabs.

In his second expedition to the Auckland Islands to search for the *General Grant*, Kelly Tarlton teamed up in 1975 with 40-year-old Royal Navy man Commander John Grattan, OBE. Grattan had been diving since 1955: according to the *Evening Post*, 'he has been credited with salvaging more ancient wrecks than any other man.' It was reported that Commander Grattan had been responsible for finding the Spanish Galleon *Santa Maria de la Rosa* off the Irish coast with a vast amount of treasure on board. When Grattan had visited New Zealand on HMS *Fife* in 1974 he had claimed that for a fee of $30,000 he could recover $4,000,000 worth of gold. The 1975 venture was backed by Christchurch financier Gerald O'Farrell, who had reputedly spent $120,000.⁴

The expedition set out on RV *Acheron*, under skipper Alex Black, with high hopes and the blessing of fine weather. They possessed what they felt was potentially a great help in their search. That was the diary of Putwain, who had been the diver on the 1868 *Southland* expedition, with James Teer as guide.

Once at the Auckland Islands, the expedition's divers searched for and found the wreck of the *Dundonald*, which had been wrecked on Disappointment Island in 1907. They hoped that if the *Dundonald*'s remains could be found intact there was a good chance of finding the wreck of the elusive *General Grant*.

Three days after the *Acheron* arrived at the Auckland Islands and made the initial exploratory dives on the *Dundonald*, diver John Dearling was the first to find an unknown wreck, though this honour was reputedly later claimed by others. He discovered a large piece of iron, a piece of a rudder, wedged in a rock 30 feet below the surface. Then Kelly Tarlton and Malcolm Blair found four anchors, a windlass, bollards, capstans and mast bands; the anchors were in the stowed position, as described by the survivors. Had they found the *General Grant*?

Initially Kelly Tarlton was reported as saying that he was 'almost certain' that the wreck found was that of the *General Grant*, while

Commander Grattan felt '95% certain' of their find.[5] One apparently compelling piece of evidence came when they measured the length of the wreck: from the anchors in the bow to the bollards at the stern it was found to be 179 feet 6 inches and the *General Grant* was known to have been 180 feet long. This measurement was checked by Alex Black, skipper of the *Acheron*.[6] One would not have to be too much of a sceptic to question whether a wooden ship wrecked on an iron-bound coast in some of the most inhospitable waters in the world 119 years earlier could be measured to within six inches. Relics from the vessel brought back to New Zealand included the top of a ship's bell, the base of a ship's compass, a piece of bilge pump and some decorative French tiles.[7]

Already, however, some were saying that there was too much metal around the site for the *General Grant*, a wooden ship, but others remembered that she had been reinforced in the States with 80 tons of metal to cope with sailing conditions around Cape Horn. Before the expedition had time to confirm their find and search for the gold, Grattan's three weeks of leave from the Navy were up and he had to return to England. Grattan was the only one of the crew with a foreign-going Master's ticket and when he departed, the expedition came to an end.

In October 1975 Kelly Tarlton revised his earlier view and declared that he did not believe the wreck they had found was that of the *General Grant*. There was room for another adventure.

In August 1975, the financier O'Farrell was declared bankrupt in the New Zealand Supreme Court but his wife Heather was a principal in the next *General Grant* syndicate, Archaeological Holdings, along with Grattan and James (Jim) Higginson. The latter described himself as a novelist who planned to write a book and make a television documentary about the expedition. He subsequently did both, under the shared title *Yesterday's Gold*. It is possible that he had a financial interest in this expedition as he is referred to in the media as 'leader', but that may only have been of the film crew.

By now the value of gold had skyrocketed and the *New Zealand Herald* reported that the new expedition 'expects to rake in well over $40 million, after British backers are paid off, and expenses and various other charges are met'. Grattan was quoted as saying 'that's if we recover all the bullion reputed to be on board. There could be more of course.'[8] This optimistic figure was made all the more attractive by the fact that the group was reported to have negotiated a deal with the New Zealand government that would allow it to keep 90 per cent of the value of the gold found.

Grattan described the *General Grant* as 'the Everest of Marine Salvage'. When he was asked about the prospect of becoming a multimillionaire overnight, he stated that it mattered little to him and that his great dreams were of finding the guns of Lord Nelson's HMS *Revenge* and, most importantly, the great man's lost telescope. 'That's what I really want to find. It's on the seabed. I know where but I'll not tell a soul.'[9] Grattan agreed that he and Tarlton differed over whether the wreck they had found the previous year was in fact the *General Grant*. Although Kelly Tarlton was not a financial member of the syndicate, the press approached him regularly for comment because he was a recognised authority on New Zealand shipwrecks and there was some good-natured banter between Tarlton and Grattan as to who was right. Tarlton later gave the *Herald* a whole list of reasons why he believed the vessel was not the *General Grant*. 'If John Grattan finds the gold I will buy him a magnum of Champagne and I will probably have to eat my hat as well.'[10]

RV *Acheron* left Dunedin on 4 January 1976. Among those on board were the two Liverpool Irish divers Terry and Joe McCormack who had been founder members of the British Underwater Archaeological Society and had been on the 1975 *Grant* expedition. The *Acheron* was later followed down to the Aucklands by the Bluff oyster boat *Golden Harvest* carrying a number of passengers, including a New Zealand film crew (who had been hired to make a 50-minute documentary for Television One). TV1 reputedly paid $20,000 for the exclusive rights to the expedition, even if no gold was found. By this time the gold was valued at a staggering $NZ50 million.

On 9 January, when the *Acheron* was off the search site, a mysterious vessel was seen approaching from the direction of Disappointment Island; when spotted, it made off at high speed. A fishing boat of the type commonly called a Chatham Islands submarine, it had no visible name and the registration number on the bow had been roughly painted out. The *Acheron* gave chase and overhauled the mystery vessel. When asked what they were doing the crew members said, 'Having a look round', 'Doing a bit of fishing', 'On holiday in the South Pacific'. Commander Grattan is reported to have described the crew of the *Atlantis*, as the vessel turned out to be called, as 'pirates'. 'I didn't come 12,000 miles to be cut out by a couple of interlopers,' he announced.[11]

The *Atlantis*, a 43-foot Bluff fishing boat, had secretly left Bluff on 1 January. To beat the regulations, she had been deregistered as a fishing boat and declared a yacht. She carried a crew of six and the expedition was believed to be guided by a clairvoyant from Gore who was a member of the Southland syndicate. [12] This person later pointed out the exact spot where the *General Grant* sank, which was a different place from where Grattan had been searching. Since the *Atlantis* did not have landing rights on the Aucklands, the crew radioed the New Zealand Department of Lands and Survey for permission to land and obtain fresh water, which was granted. When the *Atlantis* arrived back in Bluff on 12 January, Peter Tait, the skipper, categorically denied that they had been treasure hunting. [13] The Superintendent of Mercantile Marine, P.J. Williams, gave the owner Vere Murdoch 24 hours to report to him concerning a possible illegal voyage. After some investigation it was announced on 24 January 1976 that the department would not prosecute the owner or crew of the *Atlantis*.

Grattan's strategy focused on the use of lifting bags, which could cope with 1½ tons, to move the enormous rocks that had fallen on the site they had found the previous year. The site was described by the reporters on the expedition as 'a cross between a landslide and a scrapheap'. [14] The disappointment must have been tremendous when, after having moved between 15 and 20 tons of rock, only sand was found beneath. However, when Grattan returned to New Zealand ahead of the *Acheron* in late January aboard the *Golden Harvest*, he was still very buoyant and stated his belief that the 'declared size of the Gold is two house-bricks and the undeclared gold is the size of a coffee table'. [15] This hyperbole was not based on anything other than blind faith and perhaps the hope of luring investors into his next expedition to find the *General Grant*.

Bad weather forced the return of the expedition on 22 January 1976. Their only prizes were part of a chronometer or clock, a coat hook, a key (which would play an important role in a later proposed expedition), a clock hand and several pieces of a ship's bell. Commander Grattan and some others still believed they had at last found the *General Grant*; others on the expedition were not so sure.

Christchurch entrepreneur Brooke McKenzie, who is probably best remembered in New Zealand for his several later attempts to run a fast ferry service between the North and South Islands, was just 29 when he teamed up with Timaru fisherman John Baxter to search for the *General Grant*. Baxter's fishing trawler *Seafarer* had been deemed unseaworthy and banned from sailing by the Ministry of Transport. It lacked a certificate of survey and its navigational, lifesaving and other safety equipment was not up to standard. Undeterred, Baxter and McKenzie sailed anyway on 25 March 1977, with Invercargill skipper Roy Milford.

During their time at the islands they claimed to have found a wreck and recovered a plate from the site with the date 1862 on it. They also took moving footage and photographs of several other objects but nothing else was removed. When the *Seafarer* returned to New Zealand in late April 1977 a writ of attachment was nailed to the mast for a number of debts to local companies for repairs to the vessel. Some years later Baxter recalled, 'We got done for it when we got home' and indeed they did. He, McKenzie and a third unidentified man were convicted of being 'party to sending the Commonwealth ship *Seafarer* to sea in such an unseaworthy state that the lives of the persons on board were likely to be thereby endangered'.[16] Baxter's boat was impounded by the finance company and the incident cost him everything he had – by his own estimation, roughly a quarter of a million dollars. 'That was my own fault. It wasn't Brooke McKenzie's fault.'[17] Based on underwater footage of the wreck shown on television, Kelly Tarlton wrote to John Baxter congratulating him on finding the wreck of the *General Grant*.[18]

Early in 1978 an Otago-Southland syndicate, Atlantis Underwater Salvage Group, which included Trevor Lee, Doug Hunter and Lance Hunter, announced that it was planning a $500,000 expedition to the Auckland Islands using the former ocean-going salvage tug *Otago*. Their equipment was to include heavy lifting gear, a helicopter pad, a sluice box and a diving cage. They planned to use a helicopter for transport, photography and safety. They also planned to produce a film and write a book about the expedition. Some of those involved in this proposed expedition had been involved in the 1976 *Atlantis* expedition. It was reported in the media that Kelly Tarlton was involved with this expedition. The *Otago* was scheduled to go to the Auckland Islands first to search for the *General Grant*, then to help the American treasure salvor Mel Fisher work on the wreck of the *Nuestra Senora de Atocha* before heading for the Atlantic where the wreck of a frigate lost in 1799 would focus their attention.[19]

Trevor Lee was not new to gold-seeking. Back in late January 1976 he had accepted an Auckland man's offer of a well-equipped 80-foot boat to go to the Auckland Islands. The venture, which was to include the anonymous clairvoyant who had been on the first *Atlantis* expedition, had apparently not gone ahead. There was also a report in the *Southland Times* of 27 December 1978 that two expeditions were planned, both of them involving Roy Milford who had skippered the *Seafarer* in 1977. There is no record that either of these proposed expeditions ever left port.

In January 1983 it was announced that Kelly Tarlton had teamed up with Ian Lockley of Pacific Salvage Ltd, based in Fiji, as co-leaders of a further expedition to search for the elusive *Grant*. The expedition was well planned and co-ordinated, even to the point of having an expedition philatelic envelope printed as a fundraiser, as Percy Catling had done in 1915-16. Their main vessel was the 310-tonne *Pacific Salvor*, which was scheduled to leave Bluff on 18 February 1983, and their secondary vessel was Tarlton's 7-metre jet boat *Discoverer II*. The *Pacific Salvor* was well equipped and carried a recompression chamber.

When word of this proposed expedition reached John Grattan, he was reported to be seeking legal advice regarding his rights to the wreck: 'I discovered her. Of course, I have claims over the ship in international law.' But as we have seen, the wreck in question had in fact been 'discovered' by John Dearling in 1975.

At the time of the announcement of the new expedition to the Auckland Islands, Kelly Tarlton was involved in diving on the wreck of the SS *Tasmania* off the Mahia Peninsula (on the east coast of the North Island). He is reported as saying: 'John Grattan's permit to look for and salvage the *General Grant* had been rescinded in 1976.' The headline 'Treasure Hunt Could End Up in Ownership Wrangles'[20] sums it up. John Grattan, who had just returned from treasure hunting in South America, said he had no immediate plans to return to the site of the Auckland Islands wreck discovered in 1975.

The potential legal wrangle never eventuated as the expedition was postponed because of bad weather. Kelly Tarlton was quoted as saying that 'weather experts held out little chance of more favourable conditions in the Auckland Islands before April'.[21]

In the end, Kelly Tarlton never did make it back to the Auckland Islands. His energies were directed towards what is arguably his most enduring legacy, Kelly Tarlton's Underwater World, an aquarium complex which opened in Auckland on 25 January 1985 to critical acclaim. However, the enjoyment he must have had in seeing his vision realised was shortlived, as he died on St Patrick's Day, 17 March 1985. His dream of finding the *General Grant* died with him.

⚓

In January 1986 Malcolm Blair, who had been a member of the Tarlton and Grattan expeditions, took a team down to the Aucklands aboard the *Little Mermaid*, a 75-foot steel-hulled catamaran. Eleven years after his 1975 voyage with Commander Grattan, Blair joined forces with a number of mates to return to the 1975 find, which still remained unidentified. This time they were going with heavy equipment, winches strong enough to lift the boulders from the sea floor and high-pressure hoses to move the sand beneath. The *Little Mermaid* also carried a 20-foot aluminium barge called *Neptune* equipped with powerful jet-blasting pumps, a large suction device and a recompression chamber.[22]

They spent several weeks working on the site, only to find evidence that included a screw with metric threading, which was not used in the United States when the *General Grant* was built, and a small French-made brass plaque bearing the name 'Nantes'.[23] When they came upon a metal rudder, gland nuts and a shaft section, further research confirmed that they had found the *Anjou*, a French vessel wrecked on Bristow Point (sometimes called Cape Bristow) in 1905: all 22 crew were saved. The *Anjou* wreck site was about five miles south-west along the coast from where it was traditionally believed that the *General Grant* had foundered. The 1975 Grattan expedition had measured the wreck as 179 feet 6 inches long, but what was now clearly the *Anjou* was in fact 265 feet in length.

Divers then swam the coast until diver Willie Bullock found a 30-pound deep-sea sounding lead which marked the site of another wreck, where they discovered three anchors, two cannon and a Victorian surgeon's lancet case, which Sothebys of London dated between 1790 and 1810. Part of a bell was recovered, but without any markings. But the most significant find was 61 half-crowns and two copper coins, all of which were dated between 1810 and 1833: this came to be known as the 'Half Crown Wreck'. It would not be unusual for a distant colony to be using coins that were considerably older than the current date, but it is reasonable to expect that there would have been at least some currently dated coins on the *General Grant*, since by that time they were minting coins in Australia. The 'Half Crown Wreck' site had a lot more large rocks and it was felt that it would take another expedition with different equipment to discover its secrets.

A number of familiar names crop up in the list of members of the Sea Search syndicate that was launched in 1994.[24] John Baxter, Brooke McKenzie and John Grattan all reappear in the list of 15 businessmen who were determined to find the *General Grant* once and for all. The syndicate was organised by John Baxter, and originally fronted by John Grattan, with leader Mel Fisher, the well-known American treasure hunter who in 1985 had salvaged the fabulous treasure of the *Atocha*, which sank in 1662 off the Florida Keys.[25] Behind this group was a Christchurch private investigator, Ashley Keith, who optimistically told the *New Zealand Herald* on 30 January 1995, 'If we fail nobody will ever get that ship up. You may as well leave it to the history books.'

This expedition would use two vessels: the 107-foot ex-navy patrol boat *Hawea* as a base, and the 25-foot converted fishing boat *Seafarer* for the diving. Twenty-five people, mainly divers, would be involved on site. Undersea exploration equipment technology had developed tremendously, and costs had soared. The organisers estimated that to get the 14 days of decent diving weather they would have to be prepared to spend six months on site, and would need $NZ3,800,000 to fund the project. A public issue of shares was offered in February 1995, with a minimum purchase of 500 $1 shares. Television advertising and the production of a prospectus that would have done a blue chip company proud emptied the bank account of the initial $230,000 put up by the syndicate.

An unfortunate and somewhat bizarre publicity stunt backfired when Grattan displayed the key that he had found in 1976, claiming it was that of the captain's cabin on the *General Grant*. This statement was apparently intended to demonstrate that the *General Grant* wreck was relatively intact and the gold was easily recoverable. It may have persuaded the odd naive romantic, who believed that shipwrecks sit beautifully intact on the seabed, but to anyone with a knowledge of wooden vessels wrecked in such inhospitable waters as those surrounding the Auckland Islands, this was patent nonsense.

By 22 March 1995, one of the directors was telling the *Herald* that 'public subscriptions had fallen short and the hunt was now on in New Zealand and overseas for a private backer'. The money trickled in but concerns began to grow about any chance of success, let alone departure: time was of the essence as their permit was good until the end of September, only six months away. Keith was to blame bad advice from his bankers, who, he said, had recommended that they not list the shares, thus losing the opportunity of profit through trading. He also felt that negative comments on the *Holmes* television show turned people against the project. Steve Locker-Lampson, a well-known authority on New Zealand shipwrecks, had very effectively challenged Commander Grattan on a number of crucial technical points. Keith complained that Sea Search representatives were never given the opportunity to tell their side of the story. At this point Grattan pulled out of the project.

Grattan was not the only one who baled out – no more was heard of the American expert Mel Fisher. Now under the leadership of John Baxter, the *Seafarer*, without the *Hawea*, set out from Bluff on 18 August 1995, with a crew of eight, including a Department of Conservation (DOC) representative, Julian Apse. The weather was so bad, however, that they were forced to turn back when just 15 miles short of the Auckland Islands.

Apse said later that the boat was 'surfing' on the waves, which topped a swell of between 40 and 50 feet. That, coupled with gale-force winds, moved the vessel sideways about 30 metres at a time. 'The waves were picking up the back of the boat and all you could see was blue water … the nose was getting dragged along.' The boat listed up to 50 degrees and waves crashed over the cabin, setting off alarms and smoke flares. 'Most of us are just happy to be alive. I've still got the shakes. Under no circumstances will any of us go down there again in those conditions. We were very frightened.'[26] The skipper, Paul Chambers, made light of the DOC representative's concerns, and was reputedly quoted as saying, 'That's what happens when you send a boy to do a man's job.'[27]

Before a second departure could be arranged, DOC pulled their representative from the trip and revoked their permit. This was a major blow, for without a DOC representative aboard the expedition would not be allowed to go ashore except in an emergency, meaning they could not get fresh water as they had hoped.

Baxter, however, was still hopeful of getting in one more attempt before his permit expired on 2 September 1995: they would set out again as soon as the weather permitted. He was confident of locating the wreck within 10 minutes of arriving in the area if conditions were right. By September the *Seafarer*'s skipper, Paul Chambers, seems to have changed his mind about the voyage and the suitability of the vessel, as he was quoted as saying that the *Seafarer* was too small for the job at hand,[28] and was to express the opinion that having looked at the long-range weather forecast, 'he was not at all optimistic'.

While the expedition members waited for the weather to settle down, a financial storm was brewing. *Seafarer* had undergone an extensive refit in Westport by Jack Powick Ltd, who claimed that Baxter owed them a substantial amount for rebuilding the engine, wheelhouse, engine room, exhaust systems and accommodation, as well as payment for the use of their premises for five months. Baxter disputed the amount and Powick issued a writ to hold the *Seafarer* in port until the debt was paid. On top of this, Ashley Keith, who had originally owned the salvage permit, claimed in the *Southland Times* of 12 September 1995 that he had not been paid the full amount of $20,000 by John Baxter for the sale of the company 'Syndicated Investments Ltd' (SIL) to him (part of the assets of which included the salvage rights). The syndicate was in a serious position: no further backers had been found and the money had run out. The final attempt was cancelled and the permit expired.

All hell broke loose in the investment community in early October when it was announced that the 135 investors who had given the company more than $300,000 would not only be seeing no return on their money, but would not be getting any of it back. They did not take kindly to Baxter's explanation that he was not returning their money because he was going to go down again in a year's time and they were automatically part of this proposed expedition. During the following year investors tried to recoup some of their losses. The *New Zealand Shipping News* announced in December of 1997 that *Seafarer* was advertised for sale at Bluff.

It did not take long for the court cases to begin. In March 1997 the High Court in Greymouth ordered Baxter to pay Jack Powick Ltd $52,000, although the company claimed they had done about $200,000 worth of work.[29] Baxter found himself in court again in Christchurch on 16 January 1998, answering to charges under the Securities Act. The prospectus had failed to mention that Baxter had already spend funds raised from investors on refitting *Seafarer*, buying equipment, cash withdrawals, other personal expenditure, wages and other unidentified payments. The prospectus had also implied that almost all of the funds raised from shares would be used for the salvage expedition. It had failed to explain that during the right weather period for going to the Aucklands, *Seafarer* did not meet the survey requirements and lacked the requisite certification.[30] The Ministry of Commerce also brought charges against Baxter, alleging that he had 'distributed a misleading prospectus to persuade potential investors to finance a gold recovery expedition that never reached the location of the sunken ship'. Baxter denied signing such a prospectus.[31]

The fearsome western cliffs of the Auckland Islands.

(Photo: Conon Fraser)

Divers on the *Little Mermaid* expedition at the Half Crown Wreck site, 1986. From left: John Davies, Bill Day (with bell rim), Willie Bullock (with sounding lead), Malcolm Blair.
(Photo: Malcolm Blair)

The dive crew of the *Little Mermaid* display the cannon and other artifacts recovered in 1986. From left: John Dearling, Trevor Davies, Malcolm Blair, Bill Day, Peter Johnson, Terry Brailsford, Willie Bullock (crouching).
(Photo: John Dearling)

The *Little Mermaid*'s barge, *Neptune*, at the Half Crown Wreck site, 1986.
(Photo: Malcolm Blair)

Bill Day at work on the *Little Mermaid* during the 1986 expedition.
(Photo: Malcolm Blair)

Diver Willie Bullock holding relics from the Half Crown Wreck, including the sounding lead he found during the 1986 *Little Mermaid* expedition.

(Photo: Malcolm Blair)

Diver John Dearling with a bell rim found on the site of the Half Crown Wreck.

(Photo: Willie Bullock)

Artifacts recovered from the Half Crown Wreck by divers on the 1995–6 *Seawatch* expedition. Items include scale weights, coins, a porthole, pieces of rudder pintle and intriguingly a urethral or vaginal syringe – thought initially to be for cake decorating!
(Photo: Bill Day)

Bill Day in his Kirby Lite 15 hat, about to dive at the Half Crown Wreck site during the 1996 *Seawatch* expedition. Behind him are Tim Horgan and Gavin Blair.
(Photo: Bill Day)

The *Seawatch* (formerly the *Little Mermaid*) at the Half Crown Wreck site.
(Photo: Bill Day)

The restless seas and jagged rocks are an ever-present danger for gold-seekers, even on the rare occasions when the weather is bright. This photo was taken at the Half Crown Wreck site, 1995–6.
(Photo: Malcolm Blair)

Miles Purchase, Sam Day and his father Bill diving on the west coast of the Auckland Islands during the *Spirit of Enderby* expedition, 2008.
(Photo: Mike Wilkinson)

Barely visible, and dwarfed by the massive cliffs above, an inflatable from the *Spirit of Enderby* goes in to check a promising cave within a cove, 2008.
(Photo: Mike Wilkinson)

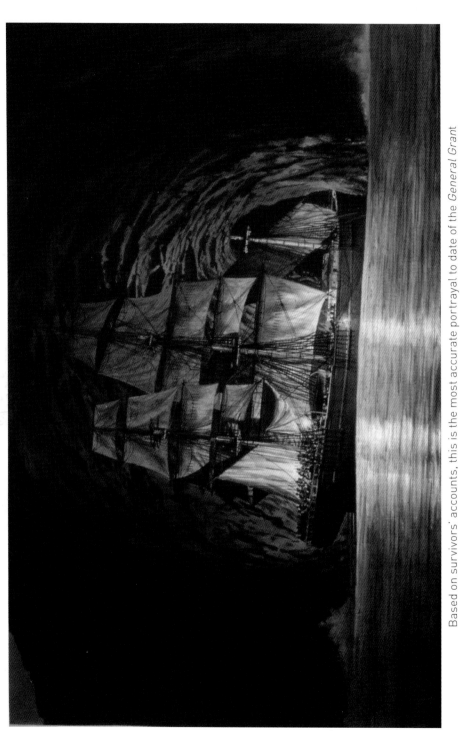

Based on survivors' accounts, this is the most accurate portrayal to date of the *General Grant* as she was lured into the fateful cavern. Note the lanterns hung over the sides.

[Painting: Mark Myers RSMA, F/ASMA. © Mark Myers]

Baxter was found guilty on both sets of charges and sentenced to 12 months in jail. On appeal, the charge was reduced to a conviction and discharge and he was released after seven weeks. To the end Baxter maintained that he had never meant to mislead anyone.

In 1995 Bill Day of the SeaWorks Diving and Contracting Company mounted an ambitious privately funded 10-week project using the 75-foot steel-hulled catamaran *Seawatch* (formerly *Little Mermaid*), which left Bluff on 26 December with a team of 15 divers and crew to work the Half Crown Wreck site. Day had been a member of the 1986 expedition that found the wreck. After the *Seafarer* fiasco, he had immediately procured the lease and also managed to get a permit from the New Zealand Historic Places Trust which allowed the divers to modify the site in search of gold, but did not specify any requirement to survey and record the site.

As well as ordinary salvage equipment, Day had at his disposal:

> underwater scooters for faster and more efficient physical searches; underwater metal detectors; underwater venturis . . . ; underwater cameras directly connected to a monitor onboard and the biggest innovation – two hydraulic 'clam shells' capable of shifting one cubic meter of sea material every three minutes. The material is then dumped on a hopper on deck, checked and sorted before being conveyed on a belt the length of the ship and dumped overboard away from the working site.[32]

A member of the team was Dave Moran, a very experienced salvage diver and editor of *DiveLog New Zealand*. As he remembered:

> Our first dive on the site was an unforgettable experience. Simon Mitchell and I dived the cave, which penetrated the cliff face for over 600 metres. There was little sign of wreckage, just the occasional piece of lead and signs of rust from under the rocks that have tumbled from the cave roof over the centuries. At the cave entrance the anchors still lay, crying out to be lifted onto the deck of a once proud ship. A cannon's shape is swallowed up in the vastness of the boulder-littered seabed. The shape of a cannonball caught your eye as you navigated between the three-metre high boulders. Steel knees start to appear as if tumbled through a giant concrete mixer and dumped from the cliff above, a twisted, tortured chain now cemented

into eternity by the marine growth that carpets the bottom, a solid conglomerate of rock.

This inspection dive showed clearly what a huge task the expedition faced: many tons of rock covered the bones of the wreck. Six firm mooring points would be needed so that the *Seawatch* could use her winches and large stern A-frame to lift up single rocks that weighed as much as 25 tons. Hundreds of tons of rocks, some 'the size of a Honda Civic swung through the clear water to be deposited on the ever-growing rock pile under *Seawatch*'s stern'. Each diver spent 90 minutes on the bottom, but the work was so intense that the time flashed by. As Moran recalled, 'we were spurred on by the ever-present possibility of finding gold as the airlifts and venturis relentlessly removed the remaining rubble. The hot water being pumped into our wetsuits kept our body temperature toasty, completely oblivious to the bone-chilling seven-degree water temperature.'

Each day more artifacts arrived on deck and then on 10 January, 'after six days of relentless diving', a gold coin was found. 'You would have thought we had found a box of gold bars. The excitement on deck was electric – was this the break we were looking for, was the coin from the captain's safe? James Teer lost 300 sovereigns – could this be part of his private fortune?' But the coin, 'still gleaming as clean as the day it slid under the waves', showed the head of King George and the date 1817. 'To hell with the date, who cares, it's gold! The smiles returned.'

Over the weeks that followed more gold and silver coins were found, but none had Queen Victoria's head on them. 'It was a very real concern. If only we could find a coin dated closer to 1866!' They found more artifacts, including a small brass porthole still with its glass, and 'Sheffield' stamped on the back. Was this Sheffield in England? They also recovered part of what could be an oven door: 'we could clearly see the cast lettering of "L. Pool". Liverpool was often referred to as L. Pool in the 1800s. We had to ask ourselves, were we digging up an English-constructed vessel?'

So was this the *General Grant*? It fitted much of the survivors' description. They were in the cave entrance, which was just wide enough to take in the bow of the *General Grant*. The wreckage covered an area consistent with the length of the wrecked vessel, and the materials that the expedition was finding fitted the construction of the *General Grant*: a fully rigged ship, cheaply built with a copper-sheathed hull and copper and iron fastenings. The location was well within the confines of where the wreck ought to have been. But the artifacts being found 'were asking more questions than answering them. The question had to be asked: were we working on an unknown wreck that had ended up in virtually the same situation as the *General Grant*? Was it one of the numerous ships that left Australia never to be sighted again? It was becoming a nagging possibility and one we could not ignore.'

By 10 February they had been diving the wreck site for 25 days, and the 11 divers had spent 450 hours underwater. 'As the weather pattern settled into a continuous series of lows swinging around the South Pole it became obvious, as the weather fax spat out the same story day after day, that as with all previous expeditions the weather was dictating the cards to be laid on the table.' But the team desperately wanted to have one more go, to perhaps find the elusive evidence that would identify the wreck. It was not to be. After spending 15 days sheltering from the fierce westerly winds, they reluctantly left, reaching New Zealand on Friday 1 March.

Dave Moran regards this expedition as the best funded, best planned and best equipped up to that time. All the divers had commercial experience and their motivation was high. The PR machine back in Wellington was ready to crank into gear but the champagne in the fridge of the Seawatch remained unopened. Most of the artifacts found by the Day expedition were donated to the Wellington Maritime Museum (now the Museum of Wellington City and Sea). The Maritime Archaeological Association of New Zealand (MAANZ) conserved the artifacts in their laboratory on board the floating crane *Hikitia* in Wellington and tried to identify them. They included, as well as those already described, a set of brass scale weights made by Avery's of England in 1826, a number of other small portholes, and a lead water closet cistern marked with the British government broad arrow. All of these pointed to an English vessel wrecked around 1833. The MAANZ continues to work on preserving the artifacts and is undertaking research in order to try to identify the vessel.

In March 1999 Bill Day returned to the Auckland Islands on the *Sea Surveyor* with a team of 11: this was to be a reconnaissance trip for a possible future expedition. The weather permitted them to work on only three of the 26 days they spent at the site – but in that time they swam a large section of the coast (about 40 nautical miles) collecting information on various possible wreck locations. Day intended to spend time analysing the new data from this expedition before announcing any future plans.

Day feels that current developments in technology hold the key to finding the secret of the *General Grant*. Because the Auckland Islands are highly magnetic, readings taken with a magnetometer can be quite distorted. The latest developments in such equipment suggest that these distortions can now be cancelled out. In April 2006 Day said, 'After three expeditions after the gold of the *General Grant*, I now know where it is not!' Then he added rather enigmatically, 'But I do have my own theories.'

On 10 May 2000 the *Southland Times* reported that Gisborne kina divers Dean and Steve Savage and Terry Satherley, with a team of 10, including four divers, were planning to head down to the Auckland Islands in May 2001 for up to a month, on a former Japanese fishing boat, the *Sea Maru*. The *Evening Post* of 13 November 2000 reported that John Baxter would not make the trip but would be playing an advisory role.

The venture soon turned into a fiasco. The crew included one Samuel Richards, a television sound engineer, who had never made a documentary film, to record their exploits on film. The vehicle in which they were travelling down to Bluff crashed near Kaikoura, in the north-eastern South Island. The chief engineer had only one leg and, it was reported, could not swim. The *Sea Maru* had no handrails and holes in her hull. Neither the vessel nor any of the crew was licensed to go more than 125 miles offshore. However, they found a 'skipper' in the pub at Bluff the night before they were due to leave and set off, sneaking out of Bluff Harbour on 4 November, before their stated sailing date, and without the required DOC representative. The *NZ Listener* reported that the expedition 'did not adhere to many of the conditions placed on them through their permit'.[33] Earlier in the year Southland Health had refused to issue a certificate to the *Sea Maru* because there were so many rats on board.

Then the *Sea Maru* was found to have on her hull the invasive exotic seaweed *Undaria*, which experts have described as the 'gorse of the sea'. It had been introduced into New Zealand in the early 1980s in the ballast water of visiting ships and was spreading. Carrying it to the Auckland Islands would be an ecological disaster. DOC and the Ministry of Fisheries went into high gear to figure out a way to stop the expedition. In the event, the *Sea Maru* spent only four days at the Auckland Islands and made no serious attempt to find the wreck or recover the gold.

On their return, the group showed footage of an old anchor being retrieved, supposedly from the *General Grant*. Rumours circulating in the diving community suggested that the anchor had originally been found off Gisborne and was filmed while being retrieved from the bottom of Carnley Harbour, in order to convince their backers to fund another expedition (the group was apparently being bankrolled by an Auckland syndicate). Ironically, even though he had never before made a film, Richards slaved for three years over the footage shot on the expedition and won a prize for his efforts.[34] It has been further rumoured that the Savage brothers made more than one trip to the Aucklands.

In 2001 a new syndicate was formed by Aucklander Joe Sheehan, a former policeman, whose career included 20 years as head of New Zealand Police Intelligence and head of security at multinational Fletcher Challenge. The others in the group were initially all New Zealanders but they lacked the necessary funding and had to seek overseas backing.

The syndicate recruited some very able support, including British diver Mike Hatcher who, in 1985, had discovered and salvaged the wreck of the *Geldermalsen*, a Dutch East Indiaman that had been wrecked in the South China Sea in 1752, with £10 million worth of Chinese porcelain on board. Dave Moran, who was to be the chief diver, has said that he was 'very impressed with the research undertaken by this syndicate and in particular the theories, logic and proposed methodology of Joe Sheehan'. Moran believes that sections of the west coast of Auckland Island are still worthy of further examination.[35]

The syndicate employed a researcher who did extensive study in Australia on the *General Grant*, which Sheehan described as ' the most researched ship that there ever has been'.[36] One important discovery was that in the 1860s spelter was being shipped from China through Melbourne on a number of vessels to various ports around the world, including London. This negates the claims that the nine tons of spelter shown on the *General Grant's* manifest could not have been spelter, which was not being smelted in Australia at that time, and therefore must have been gold.

Potential overseas backers have included some questionable people, including a New Zealander living in Brazil, and there have been allegations of skullduggery and dishonesty. For a number of reasons this syndicate has not yet been able to mount an expedition and their permit, acquired in 2001, ran out on 7 October 2005. In 2006 Sheehan would not be drawn on whether his syndicate would continue to pursue the quest for the gold. When asked his views about what happened to the *General Grant* after she sank, he flatly rejects the theory that the gold was recovered by an unknown syndicate and the idea that the vessel did not sink completely but remained semi-submerged, drifted out of the cavern, was broken apart by and spilt her contents along the west coast of Auckland Island. Sheehan is of the opinion that the *General Grant* is still there waiting to be found and that the use of sonar and magnetometers may yet unlock her secret. 'It needs to be tested with modern day electronics and then perhaps we can bring this story to an end!'[37]

On 8 February 2008 an ex-Russian ice-breaker, *Spirit of Enderby* (formerly *Professor Chromov*), left Bluff with Bill Day, his family and 50 of his friends on the now infamous 'No Fat Chicks Tour'. Day's primary aim in undertaking the voyage was to share with his friends and family the wonderful subantarctic islands which had so captivated his heart and mind, and to realise a long-held ambition to visit Antarctica and in particular the historic huts of Scott and Shackleton.

The passengers were a Who's Who of New Zealand adventurers and entrepreneurs, each of whom had paid $20,000 for the trip. Instead of the planned visits to the Snares, Aucklands, Macquarie and Campbell Islands before finally reaching Antarctica, it was decided to do the voyage in reverse order. So after visits to Campbell Island and the Ross Sea, the expedition headed back to the Auckland Islands. This was Bill's fourth visit to the Auckland Islands in search of the *General Grant*, the first being with Malcolm Blair in 1986 and two expeditions funded by him in 1995-96 and 1999.

The *Spirit of Enderby* anchored in Carnley Harbour and on 3 March two boats were prepared to take a small number of divers out through Victoria Passage to the Western cliffs to examine a site Bill felt was a good prospect for the site of the wreck of the *General Grant*. In one boat, driven by Bill's son, Sam, were divers Bill Day, Mike 'Wilco' Wilkinson, Garth McIntyre (a very experienced wreck diver), Miles Purchase and Steve Fellows. The other boat, driven by Ian 'Bish' Bishop, a veteran of Bill's 1996 expedition, contained Simon Mitchell ('one of the best technical divers in the world and probably the world's leading expert in hyperbaric medicine'), Craig Hopkins, Richard Burrell and John McCrystal.

The eleven crew in the dive boats were sworn to secrecy about the exact location of the search and informed that they were the first divers to dive this part of the coastline. Between them they dived a number of caves (of which there are hundreds) but found nothing of significance. John McCrystal recalls:

> Back aboard the ship, Bill finds his way to the forepeak and stands there by himself for a while, gazing out over the water. One by one his mates approach to offer their commiserations. He's disappointed, he says, because he'd had a lot of faith in the logic that had led him to the site he dived today. He still thinks he might be on the right track. He's disappointed, but he's not disillusioned.
>
> He says so when I ask him directly.
>
> 'You look at that film, *The Lord of the Rings*, and how much Gollum wanted that one ring,' he says. 'Well, you compare Gollum with me and you just have to say that Gollum lacked commitment.'
>
> 'So you'll be back?' I ask him.
>
> 'I'll be back,' Bill says, and the gleam in his eye says he means it.[38]

The *Spirit of Enderby* arrived back in Bluff on Friday 7 March 2008.

Each search leader has been absolutely sure that he is right, having read between the lines of 'authentic' diaries, studied survivor descriptions, meteorological reports and maps, and plotted the currents. Searchers will go to any length to keep their area a secret. Wild rumours, spread by divers in pubs late at night, even have it that on a recent topographical map of the Auckland Islands produced by Land Information New Zealand, strings were pulled to have the icon of a sinking ship placed well away from the likely spot of the wreck. However, on studying the map and archival evidence, the icon is seen to be in approximately the right location.

From the time of the earliest expeditions, mounting a search for the *General Grant* has changed dramatically. Many early would-be treasure hunters simply announced their intention of going down to the Auckland Islands and finding the gold. As time went on, more attention was paid to gaining permission from the New Zealand Marine Department and, for those few wishing to build roads across the Island, the Land Boards and later the New Zealand Lands and Survey Department, who controlled access. For most expeditions from the mid 1970s onwards, aerial photographs have also been regarded as an essential tool.

The growing awareness of the fragility of the ecosystems of the subantarctic islands and the appreciation of the human heritage created by man's interaction with that environment have led to a desire to better protect both the natural environment and the relics of human endeavour in the region. Several key pieces of legislation have been passed by the New Zealand Parliament to protect one of the most significant regions within the country's Exclusive Economic Zone (EEZ).

Anyone now wishing to undertake an expedition must obtain a Coastal Permit Resource Consent under Section 105 of the Resource Management Act 1991, a Marine Reserve Approval under Section 4 of the Marine Reserves (Auckland Islands-Motu Maha) Order 2003, and a Department of Conservation Entry Permit to the Auckland Islands under the provisions of the Reserves Act 1977. Furthermore, in order to protect the area of the *General Grant* shipwreck, which is a protected historical site, any would-be salvors must gain permission from the New Zealand Historic Places Trust under Section 12 of the New Zealand Historic Places Act 1993. None of these permits is automatically provided, ensuring greater protection for the amazing part of the world that is the subantarctic islands.

Part Three
Fame, Fortune or Futility?

Somewhere among the basalt
between Adams Isle and
the southward side of Enderby,
the *General Grant*'s gold
may, someday,
prove to be.

Jack Duggan

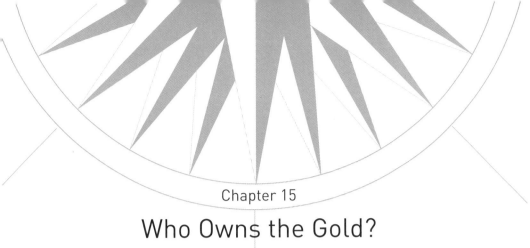

Chapter 15

Who Owns the Gold?

As long as ships have gone to sea and been wrecked there have been questions about who has salvage and ownership rights. In medieval times, manorial titles in England often had wreck rights attached. University of Wolverhampton lecturer Mike Williams, a leading expert on the law of wreck, tells of one title which included the condition that the lord of the manor had rights as far as a man standing on one leg on a rock, with his right hand behind his ear, could throw an axe with his left hand.[1]

The pivotal point in any salvage claim is the ability of the original owners of any cargo or personal items to prove ownership. If, for example, some of the 170 packages listed as merchandise, and said to have been put in the captain's safe on the *General Grant*, were found, the task of proving to whom they belonged would be daunting, if not impossible.

One of the strongest arguments for the view that there was no additional or undeclared gold on board is that nothing has ever been heard of insurance claims being made for its loss. The Bank of New South Wales, established in 1817, merged with the Commercial Bank of Australia Ltd to form the Westpac Banking Corporation in 1982. But even before the amalgamation, the Bank of New South Wales had no record of any gold being transported on the *General Grant*.

Immediately after the loss, it would have been up to the insurance company to settle with the owners of the ship. No records survive of any transactions between the Tasmanian and Launceston Insurance Company and either Page Richardson and Co. or Henry C. Brooks & Company's Australian Line for the payment of the £165,000. As has been seen, Captain N.C. Sorensen, who mounted a 1912 expedition to search for the gold, claimed that the insurance on the ship had been made over to him in 1896, though the document had been lost in a fire. He was, however, able to recall its contents: 'We hereby assign over to

N. C. Sorensen the ship and cargo of the *General Grant*, now lying in the cave or on the coast of the Auckland Island, New Zealand, provided he gives one-fourth (1/4) or one-half (1/2) per cent of what ever he may recover from the ship or cargo of the *General Grant* to this company'. [2]

To enquiries about ownership of the *General Grant* gold from Ireland in 1902 and from MP C.E. Stratham in 1916, the Marine Department made it clear that unclaimed wrecks and all that they contained belonged to the Crown. As the Solicitor General explained, 'If the gold is found and its value paid into the Public Account in accordance with the law, the only way in which it could be given to the finder would be by a vote of Parliament'. [3]

But in 1916 Dr Robert McNab, the Minister of Marine, stated that the 'government had decided to renounce any claim which it might have to the treasure lost in the sinking of the *General Grant*'. He went on to explain that the minister had to give the searching company a written assurance that if the gold were recovered from the wreck and no claim was established by the former owners, 'the Minister will allow the Company by way of salvage the full amount so recovered'. The unclaimed wreck belonged to the Crown but if it was found it could go to its 'true owner' if he established ownership within a year.

As was seen in Chapter 13, both Daniel Teer, James Teer's great-nephew, and Patrick Caughey's great-nephew Thomas Fegan made a formal claim to the gold in 1952. Their letters were forwarded from the New Zealand High Commission in London to the Secretary of External Affairs, the Minister of Marine and the Minister of Customs. Obviously, it was time for the bureaucrats to develop a policy. In June 1952, the Secretary of Marine wrote to the Secretary of External Affairs.

> Regarding the indication in Mr. Teer's letter that permission had been given to certain gentlemen to salvage the gold, this is news to this department which is not aware of any statement being made nor of any application of permission to salvage. As far as I can ascertain the *General Grant* is an abandoned wreck which has already been the subject of several sorties for salvage purposes, all meeting with disaster.

Clearly the Government had changed its position on the ownership of wrecks, as he went on to explain that property in an abandoned wreck was the Crown's, 'and if at any time, the wreck was located and the gold salvaged (which is most unlikely) the Crown would no doubt demand payment of at least a proportion of the proceeds'. But even if some gold was recovered, Daniel Teer would have to prove that it had been 'in the possession of James Teer when the *General Grant* went down. You will appreciate therefore the legal difficulties of any claimant.' He suggested a reply to Teer explaining that 'no enquiry as to salvage has been made in New Zealand [and that] in the event of salvage in the future the claim of Mr. Teer and his two sisters is now recorded and would be dealt with at that stage'.[4]

Teer wrote again in 1956 when word of another salvage attempt reached the press. as did one S.C. Sadler:

> On the advice of New Zealand House, London .... I wish to lodge a claim as the next of kin to the late Jack Teer, to whom a suitably engraved gold watch was presented in recognition of the services he rendered to the survivors of the *General Grant*. The watch is in my possession.

Another enquiry came from another Daniel Teer, this one in Adelaide, Australia. Also in 1956, Mrs S. Pope, Captain McLaughlin's [*sic*] great-granddaughter, wrote from London, asking about a claim to the gold and explaining that her ancestor had been 'trading on his own account – as captains were allowed to do in those days – and therefore had property and goods on board of his own as well'.

She must have been somewhat disappointed by the official reply: 'Notwithstanding you and your sister are descendants ... it is doubtful that your claim would be successful. However your claim will be considered in the event of any gold being recovered from the wreck.'[5]

As the years passed, more complications arose as the status of the *General Grant* changed from being just a wreck to a historical artifact. In 1993 the Historic Places Act came into force, as did the UNESCO Convention on the Protection of Underwater Cultural Heritage. These two documents essentially state, in the words of the Historic Places Act 1993, that any ship, or part thereof, including cargo, which had been wrecked before 1900 is of 'national, historical, scientific, or artistic value or importance' and may not be damaged or modified in any way. Any prospective salvor must obtain a written certificate of permission before any item may be removed.

In the end, any future claims will come down to a decision by the courts.

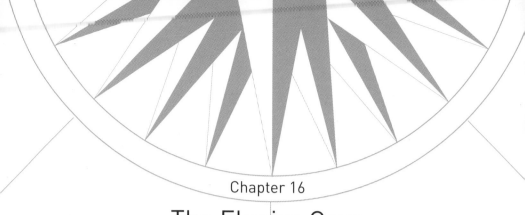

Chapter 16

The Elusive Cave

As you sail below the looming cliffs of Auckland Island, your eyes are drawn upward to the ever-changing light and shade, to the mist swirling around their tops and to the cuts and crevasses which slice in at all angles. Dozens over the years have scanned the waterline, imagining a full-rigged ship being pulled into the maw of a gigantic cave – like the amount of gold on board, the size of the cave has grown with the telling of the tale – but among the hundreds of caves and indentations along the coast, is there one that still harbours the remains of the *General Grant*?

One would have certainly thought that Teer, Ashworth and Drew, the three survivors who returned to the islands with expeditions in search of the gold, would have been able to pinpoint the location. However, Drew told Captain John Fairchild, master of the government steamer *Hinemoa*, that he simply could not fix the position within a mile. Just a few short weeks after the rescue, Henry Armstrong, who was on the *Amherst*, stated that even though they rowed the full length of the island they saw nothing that fitted the descriptions of the survivors.

Teer described the site to a reporter:

> The two points struck formed the entrance to a cove. Her [the ship's] head fell off towards the cove, and her side was rubbing against the perpendicular rocks. Owing to the darkness, we saw nothing save the dark mass above and around us. Lamps were held over the side, as the ship was lying very easily. We could then see the overhanging rocks and no place where a bird could rest upon them. Soundings were taken, and I think it was twenty-five fathoms under her stern, and all the while she kept working into the cave. ... The ship continued to go farther into the cave. She caught the overhanging rocks with her fore royal mast, and carried it away; the topmast and lower mast also

fell; the stumps of the masts touching the top of the cave brought down large pieces of the rocks; one piece went through her forecastle deck, while another went through her starboard deck house.

...while outside deliberating upon what was best to be done, I had an opportunity of seeing the whole of the cave. The rocks around it, I think, were about 500 feet high, and overhanging. The ship was in underneath these about two lengths of herself [about 360 feet]. The coast, as far as we could see, was high, perpendicular rock, and we saw no possibility of landing.[1]

In December 1954, when the British expedition was reported to be imminent, comments appeared in the press from three men who had spent time on the Auckland Islands from 1941 to 1943 as members of the highly secret wartime Cape Expedition. This was intended to advise the New Zealand Navy of any visits to the Auckland and Campbell Islands by German raiding or supply ships.[2] Dr (later Sir Charles) Fleming of the New Zealand Geological Survey said he was pessimistic because of 'the very rapid erosion constantly taking place on the Western coastline. The giant waves erode fast and carry material fast. Sand, gravel, rocks and earth which fall into the sea from the 800 feet cliffs are rapidly transported away by the sea . . . . Contemporary accounts of where she went ashore do not line up when put to the test on the spot.' W.H. (Bill) Dawbin, a zoology lecturer at Victoria University, said, 'From the shape of the island, only half of it or less than half of it remains. The rest of it has been washed away by the continual battering of the sea.' L.H. (Laurie) Pollock, who had been to the Aucklands twice as a coastwatcher and as a member of the Cape Expedition believed that 'on the West Coast where the *General Grant* was wrecked, there is terrific erosion and terrible seas to contend with. They will be extremely lucky to do any good.' All three rated the chances of recovering the gold as 'very poor'.[3]

There has been some controversy as to whether the land first sighted by the *General Grant* was indeed Disappointment Island. According to Eunson, Loughlin and his mates 'remained confident that the ship could be taken between Disappointment Island, now identified, and the main Auckland Island and sailed clear'.[4] Higginson believes that the *General Grant* was much further south, 'coming up on Bristow Point or one of the headlands around Cape Lovitt'.

In these circumstances the first sight of land could well have been of either cape off the port bow..... Unless the Captain thought he was approaching Adams Is. (and there has been no suggestion he did), he would run to the north to clear the land. Any other course would take him straight into the cliffs. While the direction of his tack may vary in the reports, they all more or less agree on the time-lapse, before resuming course and from then until the impact.

Higginson calculates that the *General Grant* could not have covered more than two or three miles – 'certainly not enough distance to safely clear Disappointment Island if that were the sighting'. From that point, the time until they saw land again on the lee bow 'was too short, even with a following wind, for the *General Grant* to have carried, from some new position NW of Disappointment east and south on a curved path to the vicinity of Beehive Rocks, a distance of 9 or 10 miles'. The ship would have had to pass the hazardous rocks without incident and the first land they would have seen on such a course 'would have been on the port quarter because the line of the coast here goes away to the South in the bight by Beehive Rocks'.[5]

The descriptions of all the survivors – masts driven through the hull, rocks falling on the decks – are consistent with the ship having at least partially entered a cave. At the official inquiry held in Bluff, William Sanguilly stated that 'the ship drifted into a cove on the coast, at the end of which was a cave, about 400 yards situated on the west of the Main Island'. Teer added that 'the cave was only a little broader than the ship, she chafed her bilges against the sides, and also the stump of her main mast bumping against the roof, which I think must have penetrated through her bottom, are the causes of the ship's sinking'.[6]

An unnamed writer who was with the *Southland* expedition in 1868 had a possible explanation for the impression of a gigantic cave:

Glancing upwards, I saw the whole mystery, about which I had been pondering, explained in a [*sic*] instant. The *General Grant* had never gone into the cave with her masts standing as had all along been thought; indeed, she had never wholly gone into the cave at all.

Over our heads was the betling [*sic*] precipice; the top of it we could not reach with the eye, but nearer, and quite within view, was a portion which shelved inwards towards the cave, at an angle of about seventy-five degrees, for a distance of some two hundred feet.

The cave itself was not more than thirty feet high at its mouth, and it gradually shallowed as it receded inland. After the *General Grant* struck on the port rock, she must have been taken by the wash on to the starboard reef, where she lost her rudder, and then drifted slowly, carried by the swell from the ocean alone, up towards the cave. When she was within a hundred yards of it her tall masts must have come in contact with the sloping cliff overhead, and that they had done so was evident from the fact that as the ship was hove landwards the rock had been scraped down by the masts. The marks there were plain enough, and they distinctly showed the progress of the ship and her human freight to destruction. When she was in the cave as far as her main chains, she could get no further, for want of space, and in that position, which was half in and half out, it was that she laid all night, till in the morning she went down.[7]

If this was indeed the case, it is possible that this whole feature may have collapsed during the intervening period, totally obliterating recorded visual landmarks. The Auckland Islands lie on the Macquarie faultline within the south-eastern section of the Pacific tectonic plate which divides the Indo–Australian plate from the Antarctic Plate to the south-west and the smaller Nazca Plate to the north-west. Pressure from the movement of the plates builds up, and when released causes earthquakes. Between 1888 and 1987 14 earthquakes in New Zealand registering 7 or more on the Richter scale were officially recorded. On 23 May 1989, there was a major quake of 8.2 magnitude with its epicentre about 135 miles west-north-west of the Auckland Islands. That distance can be considered very slight indeed: an 8.3 earthquake recorded in Bolivia in 1994 was felt over 5300 miles away. As recently as 19 August 2001 an earthquake measuring just over 5 on the Richter scale was recorded on the Aucklands.

According to anecdotal records, an earthquake was felt at the Hardwicke settlement in July 1852 and Raynal reported one in Carnley Harbour in May 1864 that lasted about a minute. He described it as 'like the rattling of a thousand chariots down a rocky declivity … our beds, our table, the very house shook heavily. We were frozen with terror.'[8]

Earthquakes of this magnitude could certainly have caused the collapse of a cave. Percy Catling's first 1915 expedition to the Auckland Islands on board the *Enterprise* found three possible caverns that matched the survivors' descriptions and were roughly in the right location. One of them had collapsed 'apparently relatively recently'[9] and if that was indeed the *General Grant* cave, then the remains of the vessel would be entombed forever. Many, however, still firmly believe that the gold is there – somewhere.

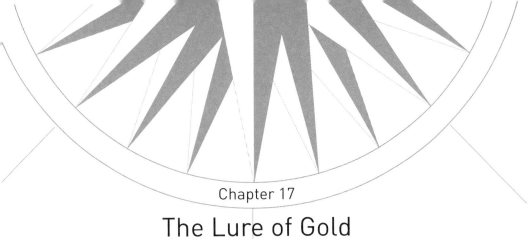

Chapter 17

The Lure of Gold

Three crucial questions have tempted, intrigued and perplexed seafarers, divers, gold seekers and researchers, fired the imaginations of armchair dreamers and persuaded investors to risk their money: how much gold was there on the *General Grant*? Where exactly is the wreck? And what happened to the gold?

On the balance of evidence, the official amount of gold on board was 2576 ounces and six pennyweight. Over the years there has been speculation about the number of miners on board the *General Grant*. An objective study of the passenger list reveals no less than 18 of the steerage passengers were miners and possibly four in cabin class (though their occupations are not listed). It was claimed that James Teer was carrying a money belt with 300 sovereigns and that others also had varying quantities of gold and silver coins, or even gold nuggets or dust.

There is every likelihood that some of the 170 packages in the ship's safe contained valuables such as gold and silver coins, banknotes, jewellery and documents and papers. Without a detailed list, which has never been found despite numerous searches of archives and libraries – at least one copy, perhaps the only one, would have gone down with the ship – we can only speculate on the contents. The claims that the nine tons of spelter on board was in fact gold, or an amalgam of 46 per cent gold and 64 per cent spelter,[1] do not stand up to serious scrutiny. There is not a shred of hard evidence that the *General Grant* was carrying any more gold than was listed on the manifest.

It has been suggested that the *General Grant's* longboat brought away some of the gold. It is said that she remained by the *General Grant* for some time, and there are conflicting accounts from Teer, Sanguilly and Jewell as to whether the longboat was heavily or lightly laden. It is difficult to believe that if any of the gold was carried away by the survivors this was never mentioned. The survivors were destitute when they landed at Bluff and no subsequent reports indicate that any of them had come into unexplained wealth. Another theory is that the survivors climbed down the cliffs, retrieved the gold and hid it on the island. Then there was the claim by Hargraves, Chief Engineer of the Auckland Harbour Board Dredge, that the *General Grant's* Chief Officer Bartholomew Brown was living in Christchurch under an assumed name. Some ask whether the *Amherst*, which rescued the survivors, later found the gold. Or was the gold lost with David Ashworth in 1870?

R. N. Kerr, Secretary for Marine, speculated that 'what gold there was (if in fact there ever was any), could have gone down with the ill fated crew of the *Daphne* in 1870 when their ship's boat and its crew were lost while trying to enter Port Ross through Rabbit Island (Rose Island) Passage'.[2] This is most unlikely, as diver James Cossar did not take his diving gear and even if he had, it would have been very difficult to operate a pump and service a diver from a ship's boat with six crew on board. The larger of the two ships' boats (which was intended to act as the diving tender for Cossar) was left behind in camp when the majority of the crew left for the West Coast. Percy Catling eventually came to believe that the *Daphne's* crew had recovered the gold but were lost on the return trip back to their ship.

Some wonder whether one of the unauthorised 'pirate' expeditions found the gold and managed to keep the secret. It is possible, of course that a well-equipped expedition could have secretly visited the wreck and carried off some or all of the gold. It would have most likely been an overseas expedition, perhaps Australian or American, as such an endeavour would have been difficult to conceal in a small country like New Zealand. They could then possibly have sold the gold in small quantities and at different locations to avoid arousing suspicion. Overall, however, this is not a likely scenario as the position of the wreck is still uncertain. Even if they had used explosives to blow the wreck apart there would still be some traces of wreckage such as ballast or anchors, on the seafloor.

As explained in the previous chapter, it is an indisputable fact that the western coast of the Auckland Island is eroding and the 'cave' may have disappeared. Yet both the *Anjou* and Half Crown Wreck sites, though littered with tons of rocks and debris, were still found. Then again, no one has yet found the *Invercauld* which was wrecked near North-West Cape in 1864.

The last real confirmed sighting of the *General Grant* was on the morning of 14 May 1866 when the survivors pulled away from the wreck in two ship's boats. Later expeditions saw wreckage on the shore and Catling found some wooden spars in the so-called 'Cavern of Death', but there is no guarantee that any of this wreckage came from the *General Grant*.

When a wooden passenger ship was wrecked, even if the hull was totally broken or destroyed, quantities of personal items were left behind. Generally speaking, iron and steel can corrode quite rapidly in salt water, depending on the conditions, as do leather, textiles and other organic material. Non-ferrous metals such as copper, zinc, bronze, pewter and lead deteriorate less rapidly and silver and gold are even slower to break down. Glassware and crockery are also slow to break down in salt, though in areas of strong current and wave action they can be physically broken into small pieces.

Divers have swum many miles of the west coast of the Auckland Islands from Bristow Point to opposite Disappointment Island, but no wreck discovered to date contains anywhere near the amount of personal accoutrements that one would expect of a vessel carrying 83 people in the Victorian era. The sheer logistics of feeding that number of people daily, which would require up to 250 knives, forks and spoons, plates, cups, glasses, jugs, cooking pots and utensils, would leave behind a large debris field. From the males on board one could expect the remains of belts and braces, buckles, pocket watch cases, chains and fobs, silver Vesta (matchbox) cases, tobacco, cigar and sovereign cases and coins. From the women one could expect the remains of jewellery (necklaces, rings, lockets and bangles) and perhaps sewing accoutrements.

Did the *General Grant* sink in the cave or was the battered hull washed further down the coast to be thrown into another cave or left on the bottom to be smashed to pieces? There are many instances of waterlogged hulls of vessels staying afloat for varying lengths of time, though in most cases these were carrying buoyant cargoes like timber, and drifting into the open sea away from reefs and the shore. The *General Grant* was carrying 2057 bales of wool as well as hides, skins, woollens, bark and timber. It is not inconceivable, therefore, that after the survivors left, the vessel was not totally resting on the seafloor and that a combination of wind, wave and tide took her out of the cavern to drift up and down the west coast for hours, days or weeks, spilling her guts onto the seabed before finally falling apart.

On the basis of his dives into the 'Cavern of Death', Catling believed that, because of the pinnacles of rock at the entrance, once a ship had entered the cavern, it could not drift back out into deeper water. This theory presupposed that the ship had remained intact and that he was in fact searching in the right cavern.

Veteran *General Grant* hunter John Dearling, who has been on three expeditions to the islands, is a strong proponent of the drifting out and breaking up theory. Bill Day, Joe Sheehan and Dave Moran, however, all discount this as a possibility, along with the notion that the gold was salvaged by a mystery expedition. To them and many others the *General Grant* is still there waiting to be found.

According to Dave Moran, there is a feeling among the many who have been after the *General Grant* that the finding of the wreck is the real aim. 'It's the biggie of New Zealand shipwrecks. We are all mates and we just want to see that bastard knocked off in our lifetime. It needs to be found!'[3] But until the wreck of the *General Grant* is found and identified, people will continue to hope, dream, plan and scheme.

Appendix I

Estimates of the Amount of Gold
on the *General Grant*

Estimates of the amount of gold aboard the *General Grant*, and subsequently its value, have varied greatly over the years. The following list gives the estimates of the value by various parties, including the New Zealand Government, although most estimates are from seekers of the gold. In many cases, they were seeking investors in their respective ventures, so they would tend to overestimate rather than underestimate.

The *General Grant's* manifest showed that she was carrying 2576 oz and 6 dwt (pennyweight) of gold. At that time gold was worth $US28.26 per oz. The value of the gold at the time of her sinking was therefore $US72,798.

Date	Source	Speculated Value
1892	NZ Government	£30,000
1896	John Aulsebrook, Sydney	£100,000
1902	Sorensen	$US 2,000,000
1911	International Salvage Co	£300,000–£400,000
1914	Shipping Journal	£400,000
1912	May–Sorensen Syndicate	£500,000
1923	Marine Treasures Ltd	9 tons of gold, 170 packages/ sundries plus the manifest gold
1934	Capt Humphries	£6,000,000
1947	Eugene Sheehy Syndicate	£3,000,000
1949	Harry Marfleet Syndicate	£3,000,000
1974	Grattan	$NZ4,000,000
1975	Grattan	$NZ50,000,000
1994	Sea Search Syndicate	$NZ13,000,000

Appendix II

Crew and Passengers of the *General Grant*

Crew of the *General Grant*

Name	Rank	Age	Origin
William H. Loughlin	Captain	–	
Bartholomew (Bart) Brown*	First Mate	–	Boston
N. Brown	First Mate's wife	–	
B. or D. Jones	Second Mate	–	
H. W. Caton			
F. C. Collin			
I. Davidson			
S. Dodd			
Cornelius Drew*	Able Seaman	–	Melbourne
W. Dutnold			
William Ferguson*	Able Seaman	–	Scotland
Aaron Hayman*	Ordinary Seaman	–	
T. Jackson			
Joseph Jewell*	Able Seaman	31	Devon
Mary Ann Jewell*	Stewardess	22	Manchester
P. A. Lacon			
Peter McNevin*†	Able Seaman	–	Islay

* Survived the wreck.
† A survivor but not on the official crew list.

Name	Rank	Age	Origin
David McClelland*	Able Seaman	61	Glasgow
P. McMillan†			
D. Mathew			
N. Milligan			
Andrew Morrison*	Able Seaman	_	Glasgow
William Murdoch Sanguilly*	Ordinary Seaman	18	Boston
William Newton Scott*	Able Seaman	26	South Shields
P. Smith			
J. Turner			
S. Whitney			

Passengers on board the *General Grant*
Cabin Class

Name	Age	Origin
William Deans	29	English
J. Edel	30	English
Frederick Johnstone	42	Lieutenant Colonel of Raglan, late of the Bengal Army
Alessandro Morinini	25	Italian Swiss
Emilia Morinini	18 months	Italian Swiss
Elizabeth Oat (Mrs)	32	English
Mary Oat	6	English
Rosella Oat	4	English
Ada Oat	3	English
Elizabeth Oat	1	English

* Survived the wreck.
† According to Eunson, p. 162, this name should be Peter McNevin (*see* Crew list).

Name	Age	Origin
W. Ray	35	English
Mrs W. Ray	30	English
Rev Father Paul Sarda SM	33	French, Society of Mary priest
John Tebbutt	35	English
John Woodrow	19	English

Steerage Class

Name	Age	Origin
Nicholas Allen*	28	English, miner
Rose Allen	25	English
Mary Allen	8	English
Margaret Allen	3	English
Josephine Allen	1	English
David Ashworth* **	30	English, miner
James Barry	31	Irish, labourer
Thomas Batchelor	21	English, miner
James Bayles	28	English, merchant
Patrick Caughey*	34	Newcastle, County Down, Ireland, miner
William Frost	40	English, miner
Matthew Hamilton	30	English, miner
John Harvey	28	English, miner
Richard Jefferies	42	English, miner
P. Kelly	32	Irish, miner
H. Kent	25	English, miner

* Survived the wreck.
** Entered on the passenger list as Rushworth.

Name	Age	Origin
K. Krentz	25	German, miner
Auguste Lanson	46	French, farmer
Clemeace Lanson	40	French
George Lanson	20	French
Emily Lanson	11	French
Clemeace Lanson	3	French
Arthur Lanson	1	French
W. Main	28	Scots, miner
A. Mitchell	28	Miner
Charles Newman	32	English, miner
Francis Oldfield	30	English, painter
Sarah Oldfield	26	English
Frederick Oldfield	11	English
Ernest Oldfield	10	English
Elizabeth Roberts	31	English
Francis Roberts	3	English
Ann Roberts	2	English
John Roberts	1	English
Caroline Smith	28	English
Elizabeth Smith	7	English
William Smith	5	English
William Stevenson	34	English, miner
James Teer*	34	Newcastle, County Down, Ireland, miner
Samuel Templeton	35	English, miner
P. Wise	25	Miner

* Survived the wreck.

Appendix III
Expeditions

Expedition 1: 1868

Principal/s: Two (unidentified) Southland brothers (or possibly the Spence brothers from Hokitika?)

Crew: Captain Kirkpatrick, H. Hargreaves (chief officer), James Carlaw (chief engineer), a second mate, a carpenter, six seamen, two engineers, three firemen, a cook, a steward and a coal trimmer; and James Teer, divers Putwain and Rowe

Vessel: SS *Southland*, paddle tug, 87 tons

Expedition 2: 1870

Principal/s: Captain Wallace, David Ashworth (survivor)

Crew: Captain Wallace, Joseph Moss (first mate), David Ashworth (second mate), James Cossar (diver and carpenter), Frank Leinster, James (Jim) Bailey, Robert Seeman and Richard Boyd (crewmen), James Cousins (cook)

Vessel: *Daphne*, topsail schooner, 48 feet

Expedition 3: 1876

Principal/s: Messrs Stevens and Taylor heading an Australian syndicate

Crew: Captain Sullivan, Cornelius Drew

Vessel: *Flora*, schooner, 130 tons

Expedition 4: 1877

Principal/s: Captain McConville (an Irishman)

Crew: Captain Giles and Captain McConville, G. H. Sherwill (diver), Dominique Farre or Sarre (diver), Mr Moffett (engineer), Jim White (steward), M. Robert, John Kerr, and John White (crew members), and possibly Cornelius Drew, a *General Grant* survivor

Vessel: SS *Gazelle*, 47 tons

Expedition 5: (Phantom?) 1887

Principal/s: Captain Bryne
       Crew: Crew of nine, diver John Pattinson
     Vessel: *Federal,* schooner, 95 tons

Expedition 6: (Phantom?) 1908

Principal/s: Captain Bryne and an expedition from San Francisco
       Crew: 11 hands, diver George Hamilton
     Vessel: *Fearless,* auxiliary schooner, 120 tons

Expedition 7: 1915–16

  Syndicate: Catling Fishing and Prospecting Company
Principal/s: Percy Vincent Catling
   Vessel/s: *Enterprise,* cutter, 14 hp Viking engine
           May Queen, oil launch, 4 hp Viking engine

Expedition 8: 1955–56

Principal/s: Bill Havens
   Vessel/s: *Absit Omen,* 65-foot ex-fishing boat
       Crew: Bill Havens, (at various times) Gus Sullivan, John Ritchie,
           Glyn Davys, John Clements, John Holliday, Peter Nye, Harry
           Green, Vernon Green, David Bowman, Paul Mollem, Ulrich
           Lucks
   Vessel/s: *Goldseeker,* 78-ton ex-Admiralty salvage yacht
       Crew: Bill Havens, Verity Gill, Arthur Danaher, Chang San Yapp,
           James Burke/Darwin Beers, Alan Addison, Robin Reginald
           Addison

Expedition 9: 1970

  Syndicate: Historical Wreck
Principal/s: Bill Gallagher, John Gallagher, Kelly Tarlton, John Pettit
       Crew: Bill Gallagher (master), Kelly Tarlton, John Pettit, J. Calcott,
           Peter Clements, John Dearling, Don Locke, Len Schearer
     Vessel: *Hamutana,* 88-foot motorised yacht

Expedition 10: 1975

Principal/s: Gerald O'Farrell, a Christchurch financier
    Crew: Alex Black (master), Kelly Tarlton, Commander John Grattan, Malcolm Blair, John Dearling, Joe McCormack, Terry McCormack
    Vessel: RV *Acheron*

Expedition 11: 1976

  Syndicate: Archaeological Holdings
Principal/s: Commander John Grattan, Heather O'Farrell (wife of Gerald O'Farrell)
    Vessel: RV *Acheron*
    Crew: Alex Black (master), Commander John Grattan, divers Mike Stewart, Terry McCormack, Joe McCormack, Malcolm Blair, London journalist Hugh Popham
    Vessel: *Golden Harvest*, Bluff oyster boat
    Crew: Roy Milford (master), Ray Hardwick (engineer), Clarrie Rose (first mate), Maui Fife, six passengers including the TV crew led by Sigmund Spath and James Higginson

Expedition 12: 1976

Principal/s: Peter Tait, Vere Murdoch (owner of the *Atlantis)*
    Crew: Trevor Lee, Peter Tait , James MacIntosh, Lance Hunter, Douglas Hunter
    Vessel: FV *Atlantis*, 43-foot Bluff fishing boat, formerly named *St Bernard*

Expedition 13: 1977

  Principals: John Baxter, Brooke McKenzie
    Crew: Roy Milford (master), John Baxter, Brooke McKenzie
    Vessel: *Seafarer*, Timaru fishing trawler

Expedition 14: 1986

  Syndicate: Southern Ocean Exploration Ltd
Principal/s: Malcolm Blair, Bill Day
    Crew: Derek Boyes (master), Jack Webber (mate), Malcolm Blair, Bill Day, John Dearling, Willie Bullock, Trevor Davies, Peter Johnson, Terry Brailsford, Chris Williams, Dave Mercer, John Gibb, Jack Webber.
    Vessel: *Little Mermaid*, 75-foot steel-hulled catamaran

Expedition 15: 1994

Syndicate: SeaSearch Ltd
Principal/s: Brooke McKenzie, John Baxter, John Grattan, Ashley Keith,
Mel Fisher
Crew: John Baxter, Paul Chambers
Vessel/s: *Hawea*, 107-foot ex-naval patrol craft
Seafarer, 25-foot converted fishing boat

Expedition 16: 1995–96

Principal/s: Bill Day
Crew: Bill Day, Simon Mitchell, Murray Rich, John Hawkins,
Pete Thompson, Ian Bishop, Jane Horan, Chris Williams,
Tim Horgan, Gavin Blair, Doug Taylor, Mike Wilkinson,
Dave Moran, Terry Brailsford, Steve Woledge
Vessel: *Seawatch*, 75-foot steel-hulled catamaran

Expedition 17: 1999

Principal/s: Bill Day
Crew: Bill Day, Bryan Dillon, Tim Horgan, John Hawkins,
Michael Zehnpfennig, Simon Mitchell, Mike Wilkinson,
Dave Moran, and three others
Vessel: *Sea Surveyor*, 98-foot twin-screw monohull

Expedition 18: 2000

Principal/s: Dean Savage, Steve Savage
Vessel: *Sea Maru*, 130-foot ex-fishing vessel

Expedition 19: 2008

Principal/s: Bill Day
Crew: Bill Day, Sam Day, Mike Wilkinson, Garth McIntyre,
Miles Purchase, Steve Fellows, Ian Bishop, Simon Mitchell,
Craig Hopkins, Richard Burrell, John McCrystal
Vessel: *Spirit of Enderby*

Appendix IV
Proposed Expeditions

1893	Principal/s: An Invercargill syndicate
1896	Principal/s: John Aulsebrook
1903	Principal/s: Unknown
1909	Principal/s: Huia syndicate
1910–13	Principal/s: May Sorensen Salvage, Captain N.C. Sorensen, Eugene C. May
1914	Syndicate: American Deep Sea Exploring Co.
1916	Syndicate: unnamed Dunedin syndicate
1923	Syndicate: Marine Treasures Ltd
1932	Principal/s: E.J. Sheehy & Co., Sydney
1935	Principal/s: D.P.L. Twiss, Auckland and E.J. Sheehy, Sydney
1950	Harry Marfleet
1954	Principal/s: Charles Levard
1954	Unnamed
1969	Principal/s: Neil Shirtliffe
1978	Syndicate: Atlantis Underwater Salvage Group
1983	Principal/s: Kelly Tarlton and Ian Lockley
2001	Principal: Joe Sheehan

Notes

Chapter 1: The Stage
1. Lundy, Derek, *Godforsaken Sea*, p. 21.
2. Eunson, Keith, *The Wreck of the* General Grant, p. 23.
3. Eunson, p. 24.
4. Chapelle, Howard I., *The History of the American Sailing Ship*, p. 73.
5. Lipfert, Nathan, e-mail to Ken Scadden, 18 January 2006.
6. Eunson, p. 27

Chapter 2: Gold
1. Victorian Cultural Collaboration, http://www.sbs.com.au/gold/story.html?storyid=32#
2. Ibid.
3. Charles La Trobe (1801-75) had been appointed the first Lieutenant-Governor of Victoria earlier that year.
4. Clacy, C. Mrs, *A Lady's Visit to the Gold Diggings of Australia in 1852–53*, p. 85.
5. Ibid, p. 87.
6. Ibid, p. 93.
7. Bonwick, James, *Western Victoria; Its Geography, Geology and Social Condition: The Narrative of an Early Educational Tour in 1857*, p. 57.
8. Howitt, William, *Visits to Remarkable Places*, p. 34.

Chapter 3: Cargo
1. http://www.standard.net.au/~jwilliams/d3.htm
2. Dyer, G.P., Librarian & Curator, Royal Mint, London, 13 June 2000.
3. Registrar of Copyrights, Commonwealth of Australia, No. 51629.
4. Hunt, Aurora, *The Army of the Pacific: Its Operations in California, Arizona, New Mexico, Utah, Mexico, etc. 1860-1866*. Chapter on Pacific Squadron 1861–1866, p. 183.
5. Eunson, p. 29.
6. Fordyce, D., *Outlines of Naval Routine*, p. 56.
7. M 1 9/12/14. Folio 1910/1442. Archives New Zealand.
8. Eunson, p. 29.
9. M 1 9/12/14. Folio 1910/1442. Archives New Zealand.
10. Ibid.
11. Eunson, p. 23.
12. *Sea Search* Prospectus, p. 13.

Chapter 4: The Voyage
1. Clacy, p. 85.
2. Jewell, Joseph, letter to his parents, 16 July 1868.

Chapter 5: Disaster

1. Jewell, J., letter to his parents, 16 July 1868.
2. Sanguilly W., *Harpers Magazine*, p. 536; Teer, James, *Wellington Independent*, 25 January 1868.
3. Teer, J., *Wellington Independent*, 25 January 1868.
4. Jewell, J., letter to his parents, 16 July 1868.
5. Teer, J., *Wellington Independent*, 25 January 1868.
6. Jewell, J., letter to his parents, 16 July 1868.
7. Ibid.
8. *Southland Times*, date unclear.

Chapter 6: Castaways

1. Jewell, J., letter to his parents, 16 July 1868.
2. Supplement to the *Southland News*, 18 January 1868.
3. Jewell, J., letter to his parents, 16 July 1868.
4. Baker, John Holland, *A Surveyor in New Zealand*, p. 80.
5. Teer, J., *Wellington Independent*, 25 January 1868.
6. Friedman, Matthew J., Edna B. Foa and Terance M. Keane, *Effective Treatments for PTSD*.
7. Teer, J., *Wellington Independent*, 25 January 1868.
8. Ibid.
9. Ibid.
10. Norman, W.H. and T. Musgrave, *Journals of the Voyage and Proceedings of HMCS Victoria*, pp. 4–5.
11. Teer, J., *Wellington Independent*, 25 January 1868.
12. Raynal, F.E., *Wrecked on a Reef or Twenty Months in the Auckland Isles*, second edition, p. 77.
13. Teer, J., *Wellington Independent*, 25 January 1868.
14. Ibid.
15. Ibid.
16. Ibid.
17. Ibid.
18. Jewell, J., letter to his parents, 16 July 1868.
19. Teer, J., *Wellington Independent*, 25 January 1868.
20. *Southland Times*, 20 January 1868.
21. Teer, J., *Wellington Independent*, 25 January 1868.
22. Falla, in *Preliminary Results of the Auckland Islands Expedition 1972-1973*, pp. 399–400.
23. Teer, J., *Wellington Independent*, 25 January 1868.
24. Ibid.
25. Jewell, J., letter to his parents, 16 July 1868.
26. Crew member of *Amherst*, *Southland Times* supplement, 20 April 1868
27. Eunson, p. 102.

Chapter 7: Homecoming

1. *Southland Times*, 20 January 1868.
2. *Southland Times*, 27 January 1868.
3. Ibid.
4. Ibid.

5. *Appendices to the Journal of the House of Representatives (AJHR)* 1868, Section E3, p. 16.
6. Eunson, pp. 109-10.
7. Findlay, Alexander G., *Directory for the Navigation of the South Pacific Ocean*, p. 333.
8. Viola, Herman J. and Carolyn Margolis, eds. *Magnificent Voyagers*, p. 10.
9. *The Australasian*, 1 February 1868.
10. Personal communication to Madelene Ferguson Allen from Tom Heard, Texas, a descendant of Aaron Hayman, 2002.
11. Eunson, pp. 73–4.

Chapter 8: Rescue Mission
1. Redwood, Rosaline, *Forgotten Islands of the South Pacific*, p. 33.
2. Armstrong, Henry, 'The Cruise of the *Amherst* – Official Report'.
3. Ibid
4. Ibid
5. Ibid.
6. *Southland Times*, 5 March 1868.

Chapter 9: Tempting Fate
1. Eunson, p. 124.
2. *Southland News*, 16 June 1868.
3. *The Australasian*, 'The Steamer *Southland* at Auckland Is.', 30 May 1868.
4. *Southland News*, 11 July 1868.
5. Ibid.
6. Ibid.
7. Ibid.
8. Ibid.
9. Eden, Allan W., *Islands of Despair*, p.137.
10. Ormsby, Mary Louise, *Dictionary of New Zealand Biography*, entry for James Teer.
11. Ibid.
12. *West Coast Times*, 31 May 1887.
13. http://www.janeresture.com/kanakas/.
14. *Southland News*, 6 July 1870.
15. Brown, Raymond Lamont, *Phantoms, Legends, Customs and Superstitions of the Sea*, pp. 20-1.
16. *Otago Witness*, 21 October 1876.

Chapter 10: Mutiny and Murder Averted
1. Quoted in Eunson, p.135.
2. Ibid, p.138.
3. *Southland Daily News*, 15 January 1955.
4. *Southland Daily News*, 26 November 1955.
5. Higginson, James, *Yesterday's Gold*, p. 69.
6. File M1 9/12/14, Part 1, Archives New Zealand.

Chapter 11: Early Dreamers
1. Higginson, p. 69.
2. Prospectus, Marine Treasures Ltd 1923, in File M1 9/12/14, Archives New Zealand.

3. File M1 9/12/14, Archives New Zealand.
4. Ibid.
5. Unidentified Sydney newspaper in File M1 9/12/14, Archives New Zealand.
6. File M1 9/12/14, Archives New Zealand.
7. Ibid.
8. Prospectus, Marine Treasures Ltd 1923.
9. File M1 9/12/14, Archives New Zealand.
10. *Otago Daily Times*, 21 October 1911.
11. File M1 9/12/14, Archives New Zealand.
12. *NZ Truth*, 10 November 1954.
13. File M1 9/12/14, Archives New Zealand.
14. *NZ Herald*, 31 August 1954.
15. File M1 9/12/14, Archives New Zealand.

Chapter 12: The *Enterprise* and More Dreamers

1. *Wide World Magazine*, May 1954 and June 1954.
2. File M1 9/12/14 Part 1, Archives New Zealand.
3. *New Zealand Times*, 13 July 1916.
4. Ibid.
5. Ibid.
6. Olsen, M.J., Papers. Port Chambers Museum.
7. *Otago Daily Times*, 11 July 1916.
8. *New Zealand Times*, 13 July 1916.
9. Ibid.
10. *Otago Daily Times*, 11 July 1916.
11. *New Zealand Times*, 13 July 1916.
12. File M1 14/4/227, Archives New Zealand.
13. Ibid.
14. File M1 9/12/14 Part 1, Archives New Zealand.

Chapter 13: For the Cost of a Letter

1. File M1 9/12/14, Archives New Zealand.
2. Prospectus, Marine Treasures Ltd 1923, in File M1 9/12/14, Archives New Zealand.
3. Ibid.
4. Ibid.
5. File M1 9/12/14, Archives New Zealand.
6. Ibid.
7. Ibid.
8. Ibid.
9. Ibid.
10. Ibid.
11. Ibid.
12. Ibid.
13. Ibid.
14. *Dominion*, 28 August 1954.
15. Ibid.
16. Quoted in Eunson, p. 149.
17. *Compass*, No. 2, 1979, 'The search for the *General Grant*' by Michael Hervey.

18. Ibid.
19. Ibid.
20. File ABPL 40/0/4 Pt 1. 1954 to 1976. Archives New Zealand

Chapter 14: Modern Days

1. Dearling, John, *Dive: South Pacific Underwater Magazine*, Vol. 11, No. 5, 1971.
2. *Christchurch Star*, 10 February 1970.
3. *Auckland Star*, 16 November 1971.
4. *Evening Post*, 23 May 1974.
5. *Dunedin Evening Star*, 23 January 1975.
6. *Evening Post*, 21 January 1975.
7. *Dunedin Evening Star*, 23 January 1975.
8. *NZ Herald*, 22 December 1975.
9. *Evening Post*, 13 December 1975.
10. *NZ Herald*, 10 January 1976.
11. *Evening Post*, 9 January 1976.
12. *Press*, 8 January 1976.
13. *Press*, 9 January 1976.
14. *Evening Post*, 17 January 1976.
15. *Evening Post*, 20 January 1976.
16. *NZ Herald*, 28 January 1995.
17. *Nelson Evening Mail*, 23 April 1977.
18. Letter from Kelly Tarlton to John Baxter, 2 May 1977.
19. *NZ Dive Magazine*, December 1978–January 1979.
20. *NZ Herald*, 5 February 1983.
21. Ibid.
22. *Evening Post*, 1 November 1985.
23. *Evening Post*, 17 January 1986.
24. *Dominion*, 17 November 1994.
25. *The Australian Institute for Maritime Archaeology Newsletter*, Vol. 14, No. 1 reported that the *Bulletin*, 10 January 1995, identified Fisher as 'promoter and consultant' for this expedition.
26. *Dominion*, 22 August 1995; *Press*, 24 August 1995; *Dominion*, 24 August 1995.
27. Personal communication from Malcolm Blair to Ken Scadden, 12 July 2006.
28. *Southland Times*, 21 September 1995.
29. *Sunday Star-Times*, 11 May 1997.
30. *Dominion*, 28 January 1998.
31. *Southland Times*, 17 December 1998.
32. And following quotes, *DiveLog New Zealand*, February–March 1996.
33. *New Zealand Listener*, 31 January–6 February 2004.
34. Ibid.
35. Personal communication from Dave Moran to Ken Scadden, 16 July 2006.
36. Personal communication from Joe Sheehan to Ken Scadden, 20 July 2006.
37. Ibid.
38. From 'Madmen and their Gold', John McCrystal's unpublished account of the trip, on which this summary is largely based.

Chapter 15: Who Owns the Gold?

1. Williams, Michael V., 'Manorial Rights of Wreck', conference paper delivered to

the Nautical Archaeology Society Conference, University of Plymouth, April 1995.
2. File M1 9/12/14, Archives New Zealand.
3. Ibid.
4. Ibid.
5. Ibid.

Chapter 16: The Elusive Cave
1. *Wellington Independent*, 25 January 1868.
2. McEwen, Mary, *Charles Fleming: Environmental Patriot*, p. 75.
3. *Evening Post*, 14 December 1954.
4. Eunson, pp. 107–10.
5. Higginson, pp. 61–2.
6. Sanguilly, *Southland News*, 27 January 1868.
7. *Southland News*, 11 July 1868.
8. Raynal, p. 202.
9. *Wide World*, June 1954, p. 84.

Chapter 17: The Lure of Gold
1. Marine Department memo, 13 May 1949, in File M1 9/12/14, Archives New Zealand.
2. File M1 9/12/14, Archives New Zealand.
3. Personal communication to Ken Scadden, 16 July 2006.

Bibliography

Books

Baker, John Holland. *A Surveyor in New Zealand*, Whitcombe & Tombs, 1932.

Bonwick, James. *John Batman – The Founder of Victoria*, Wren Publishing, Melbourne, 1973.

Bonwick, James. *Western Victoria; Its Geography, Geology and Social Condition: The Narrative of an Early Educational Tour in 1857*, William Heinemann, Melbourne, 1970.

Brown, Raymond Lamont. *Phantoms, Legends, Customs and Superstitions of the Sea*, Patrick Stephens, London, 1972.

Byron, Kenneth W. *Lost Treasures in Australia and New Zealand*, A.H. & A.W. Reed, Wellington, 1965.

Chapelle, Howard I. *The History of the American Sailing Navy: The Ships and their Development*, Random House Value Publishing, 1988.

Chapelle, Howard I. *The History of American Sailing Ships*, Bonanza Books, 1935.

Chapelle, Howard I. *American Sailing Craft*, Bonanza Books, 1975 (reprint).

Clacy, C. Mrs. *A Lady's Visit to the Gold Diggings of Australia in 1852–53*, Hurst & Blackett, London, 1853.

Eden, Allan W. *Islands of Despair – Being an Account of the Survey Expedition to the Sub-Antarctic Islands of New Zealand*, Andrew Melrose, London, 1955.

Escott-Inman, Rev. H. *The Castaways of Disappointment Island*, Reprint by Capper Press, Christchurch, 1980.

Eunson, Keith. *The Wreck of the* General Grant, A.H. & A.W. Reed, Wellington, 1974.

Ferguson Allen, Madelene. *Wake of the* Invercauld, Exisle Publishing, Auckland, 1997.

Fetherling, Doug. *The Gold Crusades: a social history of gold rushes, 1849–1929*, University of Toronto Press, 1977.

Findlay, Alexander G. *Directory for the Navigation of the South Pacific Ocean with descriptions of its Coasts etc from the Strait of Magalhaens to Panama and those of New Zealand, Australia Etc. . . . Its winds, currents and passages*, Richard Holmes Laurie, London, 1871 and 1874.

Fordyce, D. *Outlines of Naval Routine*, London, 1837.

Fraser, Conon. *Beyond the Roaring Forties – New Zealand's Sub-Antarctic Islands*, Government Printing Office Publishing, Wellington, 1986.

Friedman, Mathew J., Edna B. Foa and Terance M. Keane. *Effective Treatments for PTSD – Practice Guidelines for Traumatic Stress Studies*, Guilford Press, 2004.

Hall-Jones, John. *Bluff Harbour*, for Southland Harbour Board, John McIndoe, Dunedin, 1976.

Harland, J., *Seamanship in the Age of Sail*, publisher unknown, 1984.

Hawkins, Clifford W. *The Log of the* Huia, Collins, Auckland, 1973.

Higginson, James. *Yesterday's Gold*, Archaeological Holdings Ltd, New York, 1976.

Hirst, J.B. *Convict Society and Its Enemies – A History of Early New South Wales*, George Allen & Unwin, Sydney, 1983.

Howitt, William. *Visits to Remarkable Places*, Longmans Green & Co., London, 1891.

Hunt, Aurora. *The Army of the Pacific: Its Operations in California, Arizona, New Mexico, Utah, Mexico, etc. 1860–1866*, Stackpole Books, Mechanicsburg, PA, 2004.

Ingram, C.W.N. and P.O. Wheatley. *New Zealand Shipwrecks – 195 Years of Disaster at Sea*, 7th revised edition, Beckett Books, Auckland, 1990.

King, Michael. *Moriori – A People Rediscovered*, Penguin Books, Auckland, 1989.

Korzelinski, Seweryn. *Memoirs of Gold-digging in Australia,* translated and edited by Stanley Robe, St Lucia, University of Queensland Press, 1979.

Locker-Lampson, Steve and Ian Francis. *The Wreck Book – Rediscovered New Zealand Shipwrecks*, Millwood Press, Wellington, 1979, reprinted Halcyon Press, Auckland, 1994.

Locker-Lampson, Steve. *New Zealand Treasure Wrecks*, Halcyon Press, 1995.

Locker-Lampson, Steve. *Throw Me The Wreck, Johnny: Memories of Kelly Tarlton – The Man Behind the Legend*, Halcyon Press, Auckland, 1996.

Lundy, Derek. *Godforsaken Sea*, Yellow Jersey Press, London, 1999.

McEwen, Mary. *Charles Fleming: Environmental Patriot*, Craig Potton Publishing, Nelson, 2005.

Morrisby, Ted. *The Golden Spike*, Brolga Books, Adelaide, 1984.

Musgrave, Captain Thomas. *Castaway on the Auckland Isles; A Narrative of the Wreck of the* Grafton *and the Escape of the Crew after Twenty Months Suffering*, Lockwood & Co., London, 1866.

Nicholas, Stephen, ed. *Convict Workers – Reinterpreting Australia's Past*, Cambridge University Press, 1989.

Ormsby, Mary Louise, 'Teer, James 1826/1827? – 1887', *Dictionary of New Zealand Biography*, Ministry for Culture and Heritage, updated 7 April 2006.

Raynal, F.E . *Wrecked on a Reef or Twenty Months in the Auckland Isles – A True Story of Shipwreck, Adventure and Suffering*, 1st English edition, T. Nelson & Sons, 1874, 2nd English edition, ed. Christine Mortellier, Steele Roberts, Wellington, 2003.

Redwood, Rosaline. *Forgotten Islands of the South Pacific – The Story of New Zealand's Sub-Antarctic Islands*, A.H. & A.W. Reed, Wellington, 1950.

Sale, E.V. *Kelly – The Adventurous Life of Kelly Tarlton*, Heinemann Reed, Auckland, 1988.

SeaSearch Prospectus, 31 January 1995. Prepared in accordance with the Securities Act 1978.

Watt, M.N. *Index to the NZ Section of the Register of all British Ships (1840 to 1950)*, New Zealand Ship and Marine Society, Wellington.

Viola, Herman J. and Carolyn Margolis, eds. *Magnificent Voyagers – The U.S. Exploring Expedition 1838-1842*, Smithsonian Institution Press, Washington D.C., 1985.

Yaldwin, J.C. *Preliminary Results of the Auckland Islands Expedition*, Department of Lands and Survey, Wellington, 1975.

Official publications and archives

Commissioner of Crown Lands 2 July 1923, Ref DAFU/D311. PRL, Archives New Zealand, Dunedin.

'The Cruise of the *Amherst* – Official Report', by Henry Armstrong, JP, MPC, *Southland Provincial Gazette*, Vol 6, No. 9, 11 April 1868.

New Zealand Marine Department. File M1 9/12/14, Part 1 Salvage – Ship 'General Grant' (ship) – Recovery of gold 1884–1954, Archives New Zealand, Wellington.

New Zealand Marine Department. M1 14/4/227 'Manning of Vessels, Ketch
  Enterprise Trip to Auckland Islands. As to exempting from S and S Act. 1916.
  Archives New Zealand, Wellington.
New Zealand Ministry of Transport. ABPL 7457 Box 4 File 40/0/4 'General Grant'
  Pt 1 1954 to 1976, Archives New Zealand, Wellington.
New Zealand Ministry of Transport. ABPL 7457 Box 82 File 40/4/3, 'General
  Grant' Brooke McKenzie Expedition Pt 1 1976 to 1980, Archives New Zealand,
  Wellington.
New Zealand Ministry of Transport. ABPL 7457 Box 82 File 40/0/4/1, 'General
  Grant' Grattan-O'Farrell Expedition Pt 1 1974 to 1977, Archives New Zealand,
  Wellington.
New Zealand Ministry of Transport. ABPL 7457 Box 82 File 40/0/4/2, 'General
  Grant' Lee/Atlantis Expedition Pt 1 1974 to 1977, Archives New Zealand,
  Wellington.
Norman, W.H. and T. Musgrave. *Journals of the Voyage and Proceedings of HMCS*
  Victoria, Melbourne, Government Printer, 1866.

Magazines and periodicals

Australasian Post, 24 April 1986, 'Divers Find Great South Treasure Ship'.
Compass, 1979, No. 2, 'The search for the *General Grant*' by Michael Hervey.
Corporate Law Update, November 1999.
Dive South Pacific Magazine, 1971.
Harper's New Monthly Magazine, 1869.
Longitude, No. 23, Stockholm, c. 1974, '*General Grant*'.
Neptune's Aquachat, 1986, published by Neptune Aquasuits, Wellington.
New Zealand Dive Log, July 1986, 'The *General Grant* is Found' by Bill Day.
New Zealand Geographic, No 8, October–December 1990, 'Auckland Islands – Wild
  Splendour' by Lindsay Pope.
New Zealand Listener
Parade Special, 'Shipwrecks and Treasure' by Ivan O'Riley, n.d.
Waterline, March 2006–January 2007.
Wide World, 'The Wreck of the *General Grant*', January 1899; 'Seeking Sunken Gold',
  May 1954 and June 1954.

Newspapers

Age (Melbourne)
Argus (Melbourne)
Auckland Star
The Australasian
Christchurch Star
Daily Telegraph (Napier)
Dominion (Wellington)
Dunedin Star
Evening Post
Grimsby Evening Telegraph
Illustrated London News
Melbourne Herald
Mourne Observer Press

Nelson Evening Mail
New Zealand Herald (Auckland)
New Zealand Shipping News
New Zealand Truth
North Otago Times
Otago Daily Times
Otago Witness
Press (Christchurch)
Southland Daily News
Southland Times
Southland Weekly News
Sydney Morning Herald
Timaru Herald
West Coast Times

Letters, diaries and manuscripts

Addison, Alan and Bob. Journal: 'The Journey Home 1956–7'.

Jewell, Joseph. Letter to his parents, 16 July 1868, Te Papa Tongarewa (Museum of New Zealand).

Kirkpatrick, John. Journal kept by John Kirkpatrick, Master of the Paddle Steamer *Southland* on her trip to the Auckland Islands in search of the Wreck of the ship *General Grant* commencing 28 February 1868 to 3 May 1868.

Olsen, M. J. Papers, Port Chalmers Museum, Dunedin.

Polly Woodside Scrapbooks, Melbourne Maritime Museum, Ref. 36, 43.

Sherwill, G.H. 'Logue [*sic*] of the SS *Gazelle*: from Bluff Harbour to the Auckland Island to recover the gold from the ship *Ganaral* [*sic*] *Grant*', Invercargill Public Library.

Index